How Free Will Works

How Free Will Works

A Dualist Theory of Human Action

STEVEN M. DUNCAN

WIPF & STOCK · Eugene, Oregon

HOW FREE WILL WORKS
A Dualist Theory of Human Action

Copyright © 2011 Steven M. Duncan. All rights reserved. Except for brief quotations in critical publications or reviews, no part of this book may be reproduced in any manner without prior written permission from the publisher. Write: Permissions, Wipf and Stock Publishers, 199 W. 8th Ave., Suite 3, Eugene, OR 97401.

Wipf & Stock
An Imprint of Wipf and Stock Publishers
199 W. 8th Ave., Suite 3
Eugene, OR 97401
www.wipfandstock.com

ISBN 13: 978-1-61097-635-0
Manufactured in the U.S.A.

All scripture quotations, unless otherwise indicated, are taken from the New American Bible copyright 1995 by Oxford University Press

To My Wife, Corazon.
Maganda Ka!

Contents

Preface ix

1 Experience and Agency 1

2 Mind and Body 27

3 The Exercise of Agency 51

4 Sin and the Fall 71

5 Grace and Free Will 96

6 Sanctification 116

Bibliography 131

Preface

THE METAPHYSICAL PROBLEM OF the freedom of the will continues to animate philosophers and scientists. A huge body of literature, both in ancient and modern times, has been devoted to this problem and grows larger each year. Even so, little progress seems to be made despite the increasing sophistication of the discussion. (See my survey of the contemporary scene, "Free Will and Luck" posted to *PhilPapers*.) In this short book I hope to advance the discussion by proposing a substantive solution to one of the central problems concerning free will, which has received little sustained treatment in recent literature. In short, I propose to explain how free will works by providing a model for soul/body interaction within the traditional substance dualist framework of Descartes. In a sense, this book is a sequel to *The Proof of the External World*, in which I defend Descartes's solution to the basic problems of epistemology; however, it can be read on its own without any direct reference to that previous work.

I do not directly discuss either determinism (I have done this elsewhere—see "The Strange Case of Dr. DeVille, or Determinism and Rationality" posted to *PhilPapers*) or compatibilism. I regard the first view as epistemically self-refuting (along with physicalistic naturalism generally—see chapter 2) and the second a complete nonstarter. Since I cannot see any point at all in embracing compatibilism (or any other theoretical belief) if determinism is true, I will not bother to add to the already overly complex discussion of this position. Instead, my primary concern will be to present the positive view of this book, largely without criticizing alternative views. Given the current prejudice against substance dualism, that is more than enough for a book of this size.

In chapter 1, I make the case for taking "the first-person" point of view on human action seriously, not as a competing "theory" about the mind, but as a set of facts or data which every theory of the mind must accommodate. On this basis, I advance in chapter 2 to explain, first, why physicalist naturalism cannot accommodate itself to that data and, second, why substance dualism is the theory that best fits all the facts relevant to the discussion of the mind/body problem. Of course, some philosophers committed to physicalist naturalism but unable to face the obvious dualistic implications of its essential bankruptcy would rather embrace the view that the mind/body problem is simply insoluble. According to Colin McGinn, for example, we are simply not "evolved" enough to conceive of how the mind could be nothing but a physical process happening in the brain, although he never questions the notion that this is, in fact, the case and indeed fervently believes that this *must* somehow be the case. (See, for example, McGinn, *The Mysterious Flame*, 117–19.)

McGinn, of course, presents the standard, shopworn criticisms of substance dualism as proof that we need not take that view seriously, even though he tacitly admits that this view is the default position concerning the question. (See ibid., 118.) The primary one, of course, is the notorious interaction problem. I directly address this difficulty in chapter 2 by proposing an account of mind/body interaction within a substance dualist framework. In chapter 3, I show that it is perfectly conceivable that a nonphysical, simple self-conscious substance can influence an extended, material thing, the body, without entering into the horizontal order of efficient causes in the physical world. I go on to argue that this theory is compatible with everything that we currently know (and I think are likely to discover) about the brain. This chapter is the core of the book and contains its primary theoretical innovation, though the view presented here is not altogether new.

Physicalist naturalism is not the only form of determinism that needs to be confronted if we are to defend free will. Many Christians, both Protestant and Catholic, for various reasons have adopted one form or another of theological determinism, according to which God's all-disposing will is the ultimate, determinative cause of all things. In order to test the resilience of the view developed here, I apply it to the vexed theological problem of grace and free will and argue that free will and the operation of divine grace can be made compatible with traditional Christian doctrines concerning salvation, though not, of course, with every theological position that one might take on this issue. Thus, in chapter 4, I explain how the misuse of free will makes sin possible, even if there was no antecedent tendency to sin. In chapter 5, I argue that we can understand how grace and free will interact in such a manner that salvation is, in all positive aspects, the work of grace and damnation solely the result of human free choice. Finally, in chapter 6, I discuss the role of works in salvation, arguing for their necessity without it being the case that we earn our salvation through doing good works. Once again, my focus will be on my own positive views, rather than on criticizing theological determinism.

I intend to defend the theory of free will, which if I did not know better, I would assume that every sane person would prefer to believe if only he or she could see how it could be the case. I do not suppose that I have said the last word on this topic, and both the theory and the arguments of this book are certainly capable of improvement at the hands of others. I hope to focus attention on a neglected position on this issue, and provide an alternative to mysterianism in the face of the waning of materialism.

The second part of Chapter 1 was previously published in McClain and Richardson (1999) and is republished by permission of University Press of America. I would like to thank Karen Olson for her copy editing, which has greatly improved the text, and proved in my case to be yeoman's work. All remaining errors are mine, especially inasmuch as I stubbornly resisted my editor's advice on a number of points. Special thanks are due my wife, to whom I am proud and happy to dedicate this book.

1

Experience and Agency

FACT AND THEORY IN PHILOSOPHICAL PSYCHOLOGY

IN THE 1980s, IT was popular to describe everyday intentional psychological explanations of human action as examples of "folk psychology," a prescientific attempt to construct a causal theory of human behavior potentially in competition with contemporary materialist theories of mind grounded in neurophysiology and computer science.[1] Proponents of black-box functionalism, artificial intelligence (AI), and neuropsychology viewed folk psychology as the psychological equivalent of "folk physics," "folk medicine," or "folk chemistry," i.e., as a crude, unsystematic collection of roughly true generalizations adequate for everyday purposes but destined to be wholly supplanted by modern, scientific psychology or, if retained at all, interpreted merely instrumentally.[2] However, proponents of folk psychology within psychology and philosophy objected, with surprising plausibility, that the theory is empirically well founded and not, in fact, refuted by current scientific research.[3] My concern is not with this discussion, which in any case has long since ceased to animate the philosophy of mind. Instead, I want to challenge something that was taken for granted by both sides in the

---

1. See, e.g., Greenwood, *Future of Folk Psychology*, especially 1–21 and references.

2. See Churchland, "Folk psychology," 51–69, and Ramsey, Stich, and Garon, "Connectionism," 93–119, for the first option. See Dennett, "Two contrasts," 135–48, as well as Dennett's other works in the philosophy of mind for the second option.

3. See Horgan and Woodward, "Folk psychology," 149–175; Margolis, "Autonomy of folk psychology," 242–62; and McDonough, "Culturalist account," 263–88. See Swinburne, *Existence of God*, 35–45 and 61–66, for another exposition and defense of personalistic explanation (folk psychology).

debate, namely, that folk psychology really is a *theory* and that, second, this theory is embedded in common sense and ordinary speech.

I will argue that what materialists call "folk psychology" is not a theory at all, let alone the theory of the plain man, but instead a set of facts to which any proposed psychological theory must accommodate itself and which, I will argue, constitutes an ineliminable stumbling block to the acceptance of causal theories of human behavior. Against both the scientific materialists and the proponents of folk psychology, I will argue that their main point of agreement, i.e., that according to folk psychology, beliefs and desires are efficient *causes* of our intentional actions, is false because it does not fit the phenomenological facts. I conclude by rejecting both materialism and folk psychology construed as a causal theory about human action in favor of the view that there can be no successful causal explanation of human action, the view I believe to be the correct, as well as the genuinely common-sense, view. To begin with, let us consider, in general, what it means for something to be a theory.

What Is a Theory?

I begin by stating two claims that, though widely accepted, have implications that are not always recognized. The first is that theories are intentional in the sense that they are *of* or *about* something other than themselves. Theories purport to explain or account for something pretheoretical, at least relative to the theory itself—the entities, processes, or states of affairs to be explained. An *explanans* implies an *explanandum*: this *explanandum*, whatever it is, I propose to call the "set of *facts*" to be explained by the theory and to which that theory is responsible.

Let us note that the terms "theory" and "fact" are relative terms, denoting a set of propositions on the one hand and a set of nonpropositional realities serving as the putative object of observation/explanation. I intend no implication to the effect that the set of observations in question is somehow "pure" in the sense that it is absolutely pretheoretical or altogether free from prior interpretation or even that these putative facts be known to be true in some way independently of prior theorizing. However true it may be that theories in some sense create their own *confirmatory* facts, it is simply false to suppose that theories somehow create themselves *ex nihilo* along with the facts that they are intended to explain. Instead, the activity that issues in the construction of theories is something that is itself called forth by a perceived need to account for something non- and pretheoretical in relation to those theories, which stands over and against that activity and is at least initially normative for the success of that activity. The intentionality of theories, then, presupposes that to each theory there corresponds, at any rate initially at its origin in time, a set of facts that it attempts to model and to which it is accountable for its success.

The second observation is the widely accepted thesis that causal connections are not directly observable. It is this that makes causal claims the paradigmatic example of theoretical claims, claims that go beyond mere description and bridge the gap between description (the *factual*) and explanation (the *theoretical*), by postulating entities and mechanisms capable of producing, or bringing about, the phenomena to be explained. However, if this is so, then, in accordance with the first claim made above, the facts that lead us to seek causes must be apprehended and understood as existing or obtaining "outside of their causes," i.e., in a manner independent of their efficient causal relations to other things.[4] While there are many sources from which such facts can be derived, one source is certainly in observed regularities in experience capable of supporting well-confirmed inductive generalizations; it is this source that will concern us here.

Thus, I come to tell the old story, which, while certainly over simple, is still in its main outlines correct and adequate for our purposes here. We observe regularities in experience, constant conjunctions of events or states of affairs, such as "fire burns wood," "heavy objects dropped near the surface of the Earth fall," "magnets attract iron," and so on. These recurrent phenomena suggest to us, whether for Humean reasons or some other, the existence of some sort of causal connection between the things, events, or states of affairs observed as constantly conjoined to one another. The job of the theorist is to convert this empty suggestion about a possible causal link into an account of how cause and effect are actually connected by supplying the mechanism by means of which the cause brings about or influences the effect. Of course, for any of the phenomena mentioned above, numerous modern and premodern explanations are possible, and some of these have been defended at one time or another. Where theories conflict, we have to use whatever empirical or nonempirical means at our disposal to decide between them.

---

4. See Suarez, *Creation, Conservation, and Concurrence*, 73–77, especially 75, on the notion of a thing's existing outside of its causes.

Now, of course, a theory can often be generalized far beyond the initial case it is invoked to explain. Our initial concern for an account of fire burning wood may lead us by degrees to a general theory of combustion, in which terms like "fire" and "wood" no longer even appear. However, it does not follow from this that fire and wood have somehow been reduced or eliminated from our scientific ontology. Quite the contrary, the theory of combustion, no matter how abstract or mathematized it may be, remains accountable to the sort of facts it was called forth to explain. For example, if some new account of the mechanism were to be proposed (say, an information processing model of combustion) that was unable to account for fire's burning wood, we would regard this as sufficient reason for rejecting it as inadequate. Surely, to suggest that we ought not to let this bother us and accept the theory anyway because our modern science has gotten beyond such gross and unanalyzed phenomena as fire and wood would be mere light-mindedness.

Or would be—were it not the case that proponents of materialistic theories of mind seem to think that something like this is completely legitimate where the putative facts about our mental lives are concerned. People of common sense suppose that in making claims about their own mental lives and those of others, they are making descriptive reports of fact to which any psychological theory must accommodate itself. However, materialists will tell them that all of these claims are, in fact, *theoretical*, dictated only by a theory that has become fact-like through familiarity and hence no longer explicitly recognized as such. On the face of it, this is a surprising claim, one that seems obviously false. Part of the problem, I suspect, is that the very notions of "theory" or "theoretical" employed here are quite unclear. At any rate, in line with the foregoing, what I mean by a "theory" is something quite definite. A theory is an account, relative to a set of empirical data to which it stands as *explanans* to *explanandum*, involving inference to a causal mechanism that brings about, or otherwise accounts for, the existence or occurrence of those facts. At least as far as this account is concerned, I do not think that common-sense claims about the mind constitute theoretical claims. Further, if we examine the typical arguments given for the "theory theory" in its light, we will find them less than compelling.

The Case for the "Theory Theory"

The positive case for the "theory theory" about everyday psychological claims reduces to two main considerations. First, common-sense claims about the mind are often expressible as (or at least characterized as presupposing) inductive generalizations of the same sort that express causal laws in theories generally. This suggests that they express such laws, hence that common-sense claims about the mind constitute, or are derived from, some sort of theory about the mind rather than from direct experience. Second, we use such common-sense claims to predict and attempt to influence ("control") what other people do. These claims thus possess features commonly possessed by causal laws, suggesting that they are crude, prescientific attempts to frame such laws or at least surrogates for such laws.[5]

However, these similarities are not enough to bear the weight of the analogy they are intended to support. While it may be true that causal laws take the form of inductive generalizations, it is not the case that every inductive generalization expresses a causal law. "All crows are black" is a perfectly good inductive generalization, but it is not a causal generalization and does not even support any causal claims. Further, just as often as not, inductive generalizations simply report observed regularities in experience; even those that naturally give way to causal generalizations can do double duty in that respect. "Corn Flakes become soggy in milk" can be used either to report an observed regularity in experience or to suggest a causal connection between the presence of milk and the soggy state of one's Corn Flakes or both—and, if the latter, no doubt on the basis of the former. In such cases, it is surely the statement functioning as a factual claim that is primary and its causal interpretation secondary, as we can illustrate by reference to a psychological example.

According to Paul Churchland, folk psychology's stock in trade consists in claims such as "A person denied food for any length of time will feel hunger." Does such a claim serve primarily to report an observed regularity in experience (what I have been calling "one kind of fact") or a causal generalization embedded in a theory? It seems more likely the former than the latter, since even if we interpret it as a causal generalization, it is hardly informative. For it does not attempt to explain anything, or even offer an account of the phenomenon it refers to; it does no more than wave its hands in the direction of a completely unspecified

---

5. Churchland, "Folk psychology," 52–62.

causal mechanism. As such, it claims nothing that would conflict with a scientific account of digestion, for example. If this is all that folk psychology as theory comes to, it is innocuous indeed, hardly a competitor for the materialist theory of mind. On the other hand, if we interpret the claim as factual, expressing an observed regularity in experience, then the claim has some content and there is some point, after all, in making it. At any rate, it is hard to imagine anyone making this claim on the causal interpretation unless he or she already received it as true on the factual one.

The use of such generalizations in prediction and control is likewise inconclusive proof of the theoretical character of common-sense claims about the mental. In the first place, inductive generalizations are a perfectly good basis for prediction regardless of whether or not we interpret them causally. Based on prior experience to the effect that all crows are black, I can confidently predict that the next crow I see will be black as well. I do not need to rely on causes, then, in order to make predictions, and the same may hold in principle in the case of predictions about the experience and actions of others.

More importantly, even if we sometimes predict the actions of others from causal generalizations, we do not depend exclusively on them in predicting what others will do. Materialists seem to think that in our dealings with one another we face each other as opaque and impenetrable mysteries, relying on inference and behavioral cues in order to understand and get by with our fellows. However, this is far from the truth. Anyone with whom I am intimately acquainted presents him- or herself as an object of understanding, not just external observation and theoretical interpretation. Such a person reveals him- or herself in word and deed, informing me of the myriad details of his or her inner life.[6] This provides me with other grounds for prediction besides causal generalization, some of which are inconsistent with the claim that I predict the actions of others from causes. For example, I often predict what people will do from what they say, from the choices they make, the projects they commit themselves to, and my knowledge of their values and characters—all of which I believe to be (at least partly) of their own choosing. I can even predict that such and such a party guest will entertain us because of his witty and unpredictable behavior.[7] Our capacity to predict and influence the behavior of others does not require or even

---

6. Duncan, "Seeing Other Minds," posted to *PhilPapers*, http://www.philpapers.org.
7. Farrer, *Freedom of the Will*, 166.

provide evidence for the thesis that these predictions rest on causes and hence on a causal theory of human "behavior" that has somehow been incorporated into the natural standpoint of common sense.

Of course, the significance of the foregoing will depend largely on the actual extent to which we rely on causal principles in making common-sense claims about the mind. On any view, even mine, we must admit that there is a substantial amount of this, at least in some areas. To make my argument complete, then, requires that I attempt to explore, at least in broad outline, the major types of inductive generalizations employed in everyday talk about the mental. To this end, let me now dismiss the materialist and lodge my complaint against the folk psychologist.

The Myth of Folk Psychology

The aforementioned has no doubt been listening patiently and not entirely unsympathetically to what has been said up to now, for much of it seems to support the folk psychologist's account of the nature of our mental lives and of psychological explanation. Even if folk psychology is not exactly the theory native to common sense or the common person, it does take much to build a bridge from the sort of inductive generalizations employed in everyday life to a causal theory in which those generalizations function as causal laws correlating external behavior with mental events as their causes. Further, unlike the materialist, whom I have accused of ignoring those facts, the proponent of folk psychology can claim that his or her theory is not only aware of those facts but firmly established on them. Why, then, am I so resistant to this view?

Part of the reason has no doubt already emerged. The sorts of causal generalizations expressive of common-sense assertions about mind and behavior are largely uninteresting because they lack in content. Further, as I have just argued, a substantial amount of our talk about the behavior of others does not refer to causes at all. However, these are somewhat beside the point. Folk psychology depends for its significance on its thesis that desires and reasons are the efficient *causes* of our actions in the same way that, for example, increasing aggregate molecular motion in a body raises its temperature. That is to say, folk psychological explanations are *deterministic* explanations, taking roughly the same form as materialistic ones, only substituting internal, mental events for brain states in those explanations. It is here that I think folk psychology goes wrong, for I do not think that any causal theory of human "behavior" is correct. To see why, let us inventory some of the types of inductive generalizations we employ in everyday talk about human action.

The first sort of generalization, which includes most of the items of Churchland's list, we might call "basic," for want of a better word. These generalizations correlate mental events with the internal or external physical events that precede them, e.g.:

- A person who suffers mild to severe bodily damage will feel pain.
- A person who tastes a lemon will have a sensation of sourness.
- A person denied food for any extended length of time will feel hunger.
- A person who goes without water for a while will begin to feel thirsty.

We can multiply examples of this kind at length, but perhaps these are a sufficient number of examples with which to proceed.

Such basic generalizations are the most amenable to causal analysis. It does not take a scientist to come up with the idea that the mental events mentioned in such cases are caused by the physical events mentioned in those generalizations that precede them and that the causality exercised here is immediate. Indeed, mental events of this kind are *felt* as the immediate effects of their physical antecedents and are quite beyond being affected by the will. It is not up to me whether I will feel hungry after thirty hours without food, thirsty on a hot afternoon, or tired in the morning after getting no sleep the night before. However, common sense, while suspecting causal dependency and connections here, remains agnostic about the actual mechanisms involved in the production of these mental events and is content to be instructed by scientists as to the exact nature of the mechanisms involved.

We turn, then, to a different set of examples, involving what we might call "passional affection," expressed in generalizations describing how a person feels due to the influence of some nonmental state of affairs of which that person is perceptually aware. Examples of these include the following:

- A person who perceives danger will feel fear.
- A person who has been insulted will become angry.
- One feels guilt and remorse at one's wrongdoings.
- One is grieved at the death of a loved one.

Of course, one can multiply examples here indefinitely.

Once again, the case for some sort of causal connection between the mental event described in the generalization and the nonmental event that evokes it seems strong. However, in most cases of this sort involving human beings, the connection is not as direct or immediate as it is in the cases I have labeled "basic." In these cases, the causal influence of the nonmental event is mediated by *meaning* and the interpretation of that meaning on the part of the person who is passionally affected by the nonmental event in question. After all, passions are intentional states and only intelligible in relation to something constituted as an object in relation to a subject that is aware of and affected by that object in such a way as to produce a passional reaction or affective state. Thus, for example, it is neither necessary nor sufficient for one to feel fear that some actual danger be present in one's perceptual field. Not sufficient, because one may not recognize the thing (e.g., a bear) as something dangerous; not necessary, since one can easily constitute something (e.g., a pigeon) as dangerous or potentially so, even though it is actually quite harmless or even nonexistent (such as the giant ants in the movie *Them*, which gave me nightmares for years as a child.) Thus, when we say that someone perceiving a danger feels fear, "perceiving" cannot refer to exactly the same sort of process as when we say that someone stabbed in the stomach will experience intense pain. In the former case, perception involves some sort of contribution on the part of the perceiver that is unnecessary in the latter case. Indeed, the truth of each of the above generalizations requires that there be a conceptual connection between the subject's interpretation of the nonmental event and the passional reaction that event evokes. One can insult me all day in Armenian without getting a rise out of me, because I do not understand Armenian and so cannot perceive what is said to me as insulting. A sociopath will not feel any guilt or remorse at his wrongdoings, no matter how many they may be, because he lacks a conscience and hence the ability to feel guilt or remorse. In the same vein, I have heard that Hitler felt exaltation, not grief, at the death of his father, because he did not love his father.

There is another difference between generalizations concerning passional affection and those I have classified as basic, consisting in the fact that the degree to which I feel my passions is at least to a degree under the control of my will. I can to some extent suppress or "beat down" my feelings such that I extinguish them or diminish their strength. Thus, if one feels, say, sexual arousal in some inappropriate situation, one can generally repress that feeling. In the same way, a person subject to intense feelings of jealousy may, upon seeing his wife talking to another man in a friendly way, feel his anger rising in a manner he readily recognizes; yet, resolved to get this problem under control, he may valiantly strive to resist his feelings in this case.

The third sort of generalization I will consider here belongs to a class I will term "response." These generalizations connect mental events with subsequent tendencies to act, as in the following examples:

- A thirsty person will tend to drink water if it is available.
- A person in intense pain will ordinarily act to remove its source.
- A person who is afraid will tend to avoid the object of that fear.
- An angry person will tend to lash out at whatever it is making him angry.

It is generalizations of this sort that are crucial for the proponents of folk psychology and their thesis that desires and beliefs are the causes of our acts. Indeed, in experience these tendencies present themselves not as causes, but as inclinations to act in various ways, which inclinations are, in turn, potential objects of deliberation and putatively free choice. Just as I can suppress a state of passional affection, so too can I consider and then reject my inclination to act in a particular way by exercising self-control. To the extent, then, that my experience of myself as agent supports the contention that I have a capacity for free choice, experience opposes the contention that there is any causal explanation for human action, whether of the materialist or folk-psychological sort. At the same time, it shows that common sense, which rests content with experience, has no stake in there being any such explanations.

This does not prove that no such explanations are possible or that there might not be compelling reasons for seeking them. For the moment, let us simply take what experience appears to teach us at face value, in order to see if any such reasons arise. Our next topic, then, will be agency, as everyday experience reveals it to us.

THE EXPERIENCE OF AGENCY

In his book *The View from Nowhere*, Thomas Nagel contrasts the subjective and objective perspectives on the self.[8] The subjective point of view,

---
8. Nagel, *View from Nowhere*, 3–27.

identifiable with my particular perspective on the world, constitutes life as it is lived and appreciated from inside; it is what makes introspection and individual selfhood possible. The objective point of view, however, abstracts from all individual perspectives. It attempts to constitute itself as the view from nowhere, encompassing all reality from a God's-eye point of view. In our time, the objective point of view is most closely identified with the scientific perspective on reality.

Nagel's thesis is twofold. On the one hand, we can explain most of the classic philosophical problems, such as the mind-body problem, the nature of the self, personal identity, knowledge, etc., showing how they arise from the clash of these two perspectives, which, as it turns out, do not fit comfortably together. On the other hand, neither perspective proves to be dispensable. While Nagel is concerned not to sell the objective point of view short, he insists there are some features of reality we can only appreciate from the subjective point of view.

One such feature is consciousness itself. Reiterating a position he first articulated in his essay "What is it like to be a bat?," Nagel argues that consciousness is irreducibly subjective and hence must forever lie beyond the grasp of science because the external, scientific point of view is completely committed to the objective "view from nowhere."[9] Thus, behaviorists, eliminative materialists, and artificial intelligence notwithstanding, there are limits to what we can understand about the mind from the objective point of view.

When it comes to our experience of agency, one might suppose that Nagel would be equally sympathetic to the defender of free will. However, this is not the case: Nagel is all too ready to see it supplanted by an objective account of human action that integrates it without remainder into the causal order of nature. While making passing references to the theory of agency, he ultimately rejects it as incapable of explaining human action:

> If autonomy requires that the central element of choice be explained in a way that does not take us outside the point of view of the agent . . . then intentional explanation must simply come to an end when all available reasons have been given and nothing else can take over where they leave off. But this seems to mean that an autonomous intentional explanation cannot explain precisely what it is supposed to explain, namely, why I did what I did

---

9. Ibid., 7–8, and Nagel, "Bat," *Mortal Questions*, 165–80.

rather than the alternative that was causally open to me. It says I did it for certain reasons but does not explain why I didn't decide not to do it for the other reasons. It may render the action subjectively intelligible, but it does not explain why this rather than another equally possible and comparably intelligible action was done. This seems to be something for which there is no explanation, either intentional or causal.[10]

Thus, since free will is ultimately inexplicable, Nagel concludes that it must be impossible, an illusion produced by confusing the objective view from nowhere as it functions in action with the perspective of a Kantian noumenal self existing behind and beyond human experience and in complete independence of the causal order.[11]

The most natural response to this objection is to say that the demand for an explanation of free action is itself an illegitimate one. For if my action is free, there can be no further account of its occurrence beyond the fact that I chose to do it. To demand anything further would be to demand what amounts to an efficient cause prior to and external to one's choosing that determines what one's choice will be, which is in effect to demand that the action be shown not to be free after all. Thus, one might be inclined to reject Nagel's demand as unreasonable.[12] Still one does not have to accept Nagel's position to be strongly inclined to suppose that if free will is as I describe it, then no sense can be made of the notion. If a human action is explicable, then it has a cause and therefore is causally determined. If it is causally inexplicable, then it is unintelligible to us and at best random. We seem to go wrong no matter which alternative we take.[13]

This impasse is familiar to all students of the metaphysical problem of free will. Is there any way beyond it? I want to suggest that there is. Just as Nagel appeals to experience to establish that there is an inner life, even though this may upset the materialist's theoretical applecart, so too the defender of free will likewise argue that agency, no matter how opaque it may be and remain to theory, is a fact that cannot be evaded or ignored. That is what I propose to do in the remainder of this chapter.

---

10. Nagel, *View from Nowhere*, 116–17.
11. Ibid., 117–18.
12. Ibid., 117. Nagel has anticipated this response; I will defend it in chapter 3.
13. Nagel, *Last Word*, 115–18. Here Nagel seems to have changed his mind on this point.

First, I feel called upon to argue that the experience of agency is a *fact*, not a mere "intuition" or an outmoded theory about human behavior; that is the topic of the next section of this chapter. Second, it needs to be shown that the free will problem really is a problem, not just an illusion that we labor under, and that intentional or personalistic explanation is not so much an explanation as it is a description of an ineliminable feature of action as apprehended from the subjective "first-person" point of view. In attempting to establish this fact, I will consider the role of agency in deliberation. Third, having established the putative fact of agency, I will go on to argue that, even though we cannot altogether eliminate the possibility of illusion, there is no strong reason for supposing that our experience of agency is an illusion. As such, we must regard the experience of agency as *positive evidence* for free will and against deterministic accounts of human action.

Before attempting this, however, I want to consider one last preliminary matter by isolating what it is about the free will problem that makes it so troublesome and seemingly intractable. I will attempt to do so by reference to Austin Farrer's concept of natural mystery.[14] To this topic I now turn.

MYSTERY AND FREE WILL

According to Farrer, what we call "metaphysical problems" are really mysteries arising out of experience but involving the apprehension of unique realities demanding to be understood in their own terms and not in terms of anything else. Farrer calls these "natural mysteries" to distinguish them from the supernatural mysteries of the Christian religion, such as the Trinity and Incarnation. Each of these natural mysteries is rooted in a real, metaphysical relation constituted either within a single subject (such as the relation of mind and body) or between a subject and something external to that subject (such as the relation between subject and object in the knowing act). Regardless, relations of both sorts are revealed directly in experience and are not reducible either to logical or causal relations. Awareness of these mysteries is pretheoretical and constitutes the starting point for traditional philosophical reflection; as such, the intellectual difficulty inherent in philosophical reflection on mystery is one of *description* rather than *explanation*. Since each mystery arises from the apprehension of a *unique* relation rather than one

---

14. Farrer, *Glass of Vision*, 63–78.

classifiable as a species under a common genus, it can at best be analogically described by reference to other relations that it more or less resembles. No harm results as long we take those analogies seriously but not literally. However, there is a persistent tendency on the part of philosophers to take their chosen analogies as literal descriptions, and this generates interminable puzzles and difficulties within the discipline of philosophy.

How can we construe free will as a natural mystery? Perhaps the following will suffice. The locus of the free will problem is the relation between the *grounds* of actions on the one hand and the *choice* of which actions to perform on the other. If there is to be free will, two conditions must be met. First, our actions need to be intelligibly connected to their grounds (such as our beliefs, desires, and states of character), or else they will not be *our* acts but merely the result of chance or random processes. As such, our actions must have *grounds* that typically are not chosen by us. Second and equally important, however, these grounds must not give rise to our actions with logical or causal necessity, or else they will not be free. As such, the grounds for my actions must provide sufficient motivation to make that choice and the action it brings forth possible for me but not prove so powerful as to make that choice and action either logically or causally necessary.

If there are to be free actions, determinism must be false. Reasons cannot be causes and neither can nonrational motives dictate what I will do without my consent and cooperation. As such, there must be logical and causal insufficiency in the grounds of the act requiring some further activity on our parts in order to make up the difference so that the resulting external action can be a derivatively free one. Indeed, it is only because of this logical and causal insufficiency that it is possible for us to objectify our desires and distinguish the self from the grounds of its potential actions, mediatizing their influence in a way sufficient to make them objects of deliberation. Following Nagel, we may call this "rational autonomy."[15]

According to this view, there can be no doubt that the relation between action and grounds for action on the free will hypothesis will not be quite the same as any other sort of relation upon which we might want to model it. However, the only relations between ground and consequent available to us as philosophers are those of premise to conclusion

---

15. Nagel, *View from Nowhere*, 115–17, 126–30. It is to be noted that Nagel denied that we have any such power, accounting for its appearance in another way.

and efficient cause to its effect. From the very nature of the case, then, these can at best provide analogies to the unique relation of ground to consequent in instances of free action. Nevertheless, we are constrained to use them even as we attempt to remain cognizant of their limitations. Thus, we may conclude that, at least on this interpretation of the free will problem, free will qualifies as what Farrer calls a "natural mystery," and the intellectual difficulty about free will arises from the unique relation between ground and consequent in the case of free action. To what extent is such an account credible?

There is much in our everyday talk and experience to support this account of the nature of the free will problem. For example, the very notion of grounding in this context is ambiguous, for it can refer either to the epistemic relation of justification between beliefs or to the causal relation of "bringing about" between events, both of which are indispensable aspects of the intelligibility of the free act. If I ask, "Why did you do that?" I may be asking what your motive was or for a reason justifying your action or both. There may be either a single answer to both questions or two quite independent answers, depending on the circumstances.[16] When we speak of the grounds of action, then, we are speaking about simply whatever it is that contributes to the intelligibility of action, and this covers different things belonging to different categories. The foregoing suggests that when we use the word "grounds" in this context, we are using it by analogy, not to refer to a logical or causal relation between the grounds of action and the actions themselves.

Nor does experience support the claim that our actions have causes, at least if the usual candidates, e.g., desires, passions, reasons, etc., are under consideration. We can see this even in the simple, straightforward case of desire. In the case of other species of animals, we may suppose that desires are causes in the same way that the motion of one billiard ball is the cause of the motion of another billiard ball, i.e., by the exercise of direct, immediate influence of the one upon the other. An animal's felt tendency toward some behavior or other is immediately followed by an endeavor to enact it, unless this is somehow prevented, because the animal's entire attention is occupied by the dominant motive of the

---

16. Recall Willy Sutton's response to the question "Why do you rob banks?" ("Because that's where the money is.") The questioner asked for a *justificatory reason* for his illegal behavior, and Sutton replied by giving an explanation in terms of nonrational motives.

moment. As such, an animal's dominant desire works like an efficient cause.

In the case of human beings, however, desire is experienced differently, because we can *objectify* our desires, creating the psychic distance between the self and its motives sufficient to hold them in check, at least for the moment, thereby making them objects of deliberation. I both feel the desire for a Popsicle, say, and am self-consciously aware of that desire as just one of my conscious states, rather than as the sum and substance of my conscious life. Because of this, I am able to make my desire for a Popsicle an object of deliberation, considering whether or not to indulge this particular desire and then acting in accordance with the results of my deliberation. In that case, desire considered as grounds for my action is at best analogous to the standard case of efficient causation.

Desires and other motives differ from standard instances of causation in another fashion as well. In cases of causation involving multiple, simultaneously competing elements all of the same order, we expect that the causal influence of each will be proportional to the degree of motive force ("causal power") exerted by that element; to put it more simply, we anticipate that a stronger force will invariably beat a weaker force. Where desires and other motives are concerned, motive force seems to be equivalent to *felt* strength, or "psychic pull," at least if we are to judge by experience. However, experience also teaches us that we do not always act on our strongest desires *so understood*. Indeed, in those cases in which we exert our willpower to deny a particularly urgent or recurrent desire (e.g., for cigarettes), we typically feel deserving of praise for our fortitude. What we suppose to be the case where causality is concerned, we do not expect in the case of desires and other motives for action, because it is not what we observe invariably to be the case. Therefore, once again, the relation between ground and action is at best analogous to the standard case of causation.[17]

17. Of course, one can insist that we always act on our strongest desire because the desire we experience as being strongest need not *really* be the strongest desire in the circumstances and that the proof of this is that I did not act on it. However, without further explanation, this simply makes it a tautology that I always act on my strongest desire, since on the account so far, the only criterion for a desire being strongest is that I acted on it rather than its competitors. Nor do I see any prospect for supplying some independent account of desiderative strength that "trumps" our ordinary account according to which the strength of a desire corresponds to its degree of *felt* motive force. This tendency of the materialist to dismiss all the phenomenological evidence contrary to his own view as illusory, though common enough, is clearly question begging and

If we turn to the case of reasons for action construed as motives for action, we find ourselves even more perplexed. Of course, many philosophers deny that reasons, considered just as such, have any motive force at all. Even if they do, however, we need to note that their motive force does not necessarily correlate with their degree of epistemic or justificatory value in the circumstances. There are occasions upon which we act against our better judgment; more than this, we can recognize the force of a reason or set of reasons without thereby acting as those reasons dictate. Therefore, if reasons *are* causes, they are so in some fashion independent of their being justificatory reasons, and this makes the appeal to reasons in the causal explanation of action problematic, to say the least. We do not always even believe the views to which the available reasons most strongly incline our belief.

The determinist can sidestep these considerations by suggesting that the causes of our behavior, whether psychic, behavioral, genetic, or purely physical, operate largely below the level of consciousness. On this sort of view, consciousness (if admitted at all) is viewed at best as an epiphenomenon, at worst as an irrelevancy with vanishingly little to teach us about ourselves. Such a position makes us largely opaque to ourselves, converting nearly all that we recognize as self-knowledge into a sort of crepuscular rationalization. Such a view may be true, but its truth is not obvious and so cannot simply be assumed. There is no reason, then, not to take the testimony of consciousness seriously, i.e., at face value, in this context. Let us see what this reveals to us.

THE EXPERIENCE OF AGENCY IN DELIBERATION

Granted that our experience of the relation between the grounds of our actions and the actions themselves does not comport very well with the determinist's causal model of that experience, is there any positive evidence for free will to be garnered from experience? I believe that we can provide such evidence if we can show that there is an awareness of our agency that is part of the subjective point of view on action, i.e., action as we experience it when we are engaged in acting. Further, I think we can show that this agency is both necessary to and ineliminable from that point of view. I will try to illustrate awareness of agency by reference

---

should be challenged rather than acquiesced in.

to a particular case of action, i.e., rational deliberation, a fundamental preliminary to many instances of overt action.

To understand what I mean by "agency," consider an account of deliberation from which this account is conspicuously absent:

> When in the mind of man, appetites and aversions, hopes and feares, concerning one and the same thing, arise alternately; and divers good and evil consequences of the doing, or omitting the thing propounded, come successively into our thoughts; so that sometimes we have an appetite to it; sometimes an aversion from it; sometimes hope to be able to do it, sometimes despaire, or feare to attempt it; the whole summe of desires, aversions, hopes, and fears, continued till the thing be either done, or thought impossible, is that we call deliberation.[18]

The author of this passage, Thomas Hobbes, goes on to state that on his account of deliberation, nonrational animals also deliberate, since they undergo the same sort of alternation in desire and aversion as we do. He describes the will as merely the last appetite adhering to the action, which likewise, then, we must attribute to the beasts. What is remarkable about this account of deliberation is that it converts deliberation from something we do into something that happens to us. According to the Hobbesian view, deliberation consists in my awareness of an alternating series of desires, aversions, and passions evoked by the contemplation of a particular end. With regard to this alternating series, I am at best a passive observer, at worst merely carried from pillar to post as each new impulse washes over me. He describes these impulses as contending among themselves for the right to determine my action. Eventually, one of them wins out and becomes the last in the series, the one that attaches itself to and determines my action. Hobbes calls this "will," since it is the psychological event that immediately precedes my action and, operating as its efficient cause, gives rise to it.

Certainly, this bears some analogy to the notion of will as we ordinarily experience it, since acts of will give rise to our actions. However, what is missing here is any sense of effort or direction on my part, of will as a rational faculty or power of judgment by means of which I arrive at and enact my choice. According to Hobbes's view, I am completely passive, a mere bystander, helpless either to direct or control the alternating series of mental states by means of which my action is caused

---

18. Hobbes, *Leviathan* (1651), 126–27.

by forces over which I have no control. Deliberation is not something I do but rather something that merely happens in me, whose outcome is preordained and over which I have no control, rational or otherwise. Since I contribute nothing at all to this process, I ought, in principle at least, to be able simply to sit back and wait to find out what I will decide to do and consequently enact in external behavior. I simply need to wait until the morass of conflicting impulses resolves and then observe (to my surprise, delight, or consternation) what I will be doing next.

Obviously, this is nothing like deliberation as I experience it from the inside. In the first place, deliberation is something that I undertake to do, not that I happen to find myself doing. At any rate, I cannot recall ever having found myself deliberating in the way that I might find myself absentmindedly humming a popular melody. Second, far from being an automatic process taking place within me and over which I have no control or one which I could in principle simply observe myself undergoing, deliberation as I ordinarily experience it requires my sustained attention and direction. It continues only so long as I engage in it; if I sit back passively and wait for it to continue on its own, I will cease to deliberate altogether.

Deliberation, in the third place, involves rational autonomy and is not an activity that a nonrational animal could engage in. It is no mere passive registering of the subjective weight of one's desires and aversions. Instead, it involves rational judgment. One, for example, notes the subjective weight of one's desires and aversions but contrasts this with their objective weight in the circumstances, often noting that these two measures fail to correspond with one another. It is because of this, for example, that moral conflict is possible and needs to be resolved by a choice or decision, either to do as one wants or instead to do what one knows one ought to do. Fourth and finally, there is nothing automatic about the transition from deliberation to overt action, no mere attachment of the last impulse directly to the action itself; deliberation, decision, and action are distinct. I do not always do as deliberation bids me to do, even when what it bids me to do has the force of moral necessity. I can take the counsel of judgment yet decide against that judgment and sometimes do, especially when the outcome of deliberation is different from what I anticipate it will be. I can also decide to do something but subsequently change my mind and thus not act as I have previously chosen to do.

It is this awareness of myself as initiating, sustaining, and directing the course of deliberation that I identify with the experience of agency. It constitutes the attitude of directive engagement present in deliberation and in conscious action generally, and it makes all the difference, subjectively speaking, between *what I do* on the one hand and *what merely happens to me* on the other. I do not believe that this awareness can be grasped from or explained by the objective point of view. It is, however, endemic to the subjective point of view, which, in turn, is a necessary condition for action since, as we have seen, if one passively waits to see what one will do, in most cases one will do nothing at all. The foregoing helps explain why I cannot regard the act that I am contemplating as somehow prefigured in its causes.[19] For action presupposes agency, and agency involves both my making an endeavor and (in all but the simplest cases) directing it toward its end. In the case of deliberation, for example, I must endeavor to sort out my conflicting motivations and act as though what I was doing was under my control or somehow "up to me"—and this regardless of whether I am a determinist or not.[20]

The point of all this is that free will is a practical presupposition of the subjective point of view on action, which in turn is indispensable for action itself.[21] Thus, regardless of my theoretical convictions, I cannot act without adopting a stance of which commitment to free will is an integral part. I may not believe in free will, but I must act as though I did in order to act at all. In my role as agent, I am (not surprisingly) committed to my own agency and thus to contracausal freedom. The question is whether this practical fact has any theoretical significance. Let us now consider this question.

---

19. Farrer, *Freedom of the Will*, 123–24.

20. Wolf, "Sanity and Metaphysics," in Watson, *Free Will*, 372–87. Wolf turns this to advantage by informing us that, even if we knew that our actions were determined, so long as we do not know in advance what we were determined to do, we would be in the same situation as someone who had free will—it would still be necessary to deliberate, decide, and so on. Such choices would still be "free" in the compatibilist sense, and this, she thinks, is freedom enough; for obvious reasons, I dispute this claim.

21. Denyer, *Time, Action, and Necessity*. Denyer argues this in detail. Smilansky, *Free Will and Illusion*, 59. Smilansky dismisses Denyer's view in one sentence on the grounds that—guess what—our experience of our own agency may be an illusion.

THE PRESUMPTION OF FREEDOM

At first glance, one might suppose that it does not. After all, there is no logical contradiction in admitting that the subjective point of view on deliberation presupposes the truth of free will while maintaining the truth of determinism. Surely, the question at issue here is the truth of determinism, not the phenomenology of action. More than this, there are considerations suggesting the foregoing analysis is quite irrelevant to the theoretical question between free will and determinism. After all, someone acting under the aegis of a posthypnotic suggestion of a subconscious urge likely has the experience of agency, even though as a matter of fact, what he or she does is causally preordained and quite out of his or her control.[22] Thus, no matter how seemingly pervasive and inseparable the experience of agency is from the subjective point of view on action, it remains that it is sometimes, and thus could possibly always be, an illusion.

We cannot discount this possibility altogether; still, it is hardly credible that it might turn out to be true. For, in the first place, the illusion will not go away. If I have shown anything, the assumption of free will is practically indispensable for action. Hence, it is not like the typical theoretical mistake that we can discard once it has been exposed. If free will is an illusion, it is one that we are foredoomed to live, regardless of our philosophical views. It seems strange that this would be the case if determinism were true, for this would condemn us to a state of irremediable cognitive dissonance. On the one hand, we are supposedly convinced (presumably on the basis of rational evidence) that determinism is true, while on the other we recognize that we are forced to adopt the false perspective according to which our choices matter as a necessary condition for action even to occur.

One might question the significance of this, however. After all, where optical illusions are concerned, one's knowledge of the manner in which one is being imposed upon does not necessarily alert the perceived content. One arrow continues to look longer than the other arrow in the Muller-Lyer diagram even after one has been persuaded by the ruler that, despite appearances, they are the same length. Perhaps, but the analogy does not quite go through. Optical illusions are parasitic on

---

22. Wegner, *Illusion of Conscious Will*. Wegner focuses on such cases in order to argue that free will is—you guessed it—an illusion. See Mele, *Effective Intentions*, especially 91–115, for criticism of Wegner's views.

the normal visual habits that lead us aright in most cases and occur only under highly unusual and, for the most part, artificial circumstances. What the determinist is claiming is that the experience of ourselves as acting persons is as fundamentally illusory or delusive as it is ineliminable as a component of the "intentional stance." Determinism, then, turns out to be more like Berkeley's account of perception than the more standard view that affirms the existence of the external world while admitting the fact of occasional illusion. Like Berkeley's idealism, determinism could turn out to be true, though no doubt most of us would be frankly astounded if it did. Certainly, we would not be willing to accept it except in the face of the most compelling evidence.[23]

Ironically, Austin Farrer, a defender of the free will position, has suggested a way in which the determinist can square his hypothesis with apparent facts. In *The Freedom of the Will*, he sketches a deterministic account of phenomenal liberty, which goes briefly as follows: Although my actions are determined, I cannot regard them as such prior to making a decision, because until that time the causal factors necessary to produce my act are not in place, and deliberative thought is a necessary link in the causal chain that produces my act.[24] The purpose of deliberative thought is to evoke my subjective responses about the various alternatives considered, and subjective response has to be direct. I cannot evoke these feelings while viewing my responses clinically. The relation between the alternatives considered and subjective response has to be direct. To intervene in the process by holding one's affective distance interrupts that process and prevents the occurrence of evocation, hence of the action itself. Thus, the attitude of calculation and prediction characteristic of the clinical observer has to be avoided in the context of action, in order that the causal factors that determine behavior may be allowed to work.

Such a hypothesis may have the virtue of making determinism consistent with the fact of agency, but this does not by itself overcome the presumption in favor of free will. For one thing, our apparent ability to interfere in the process by taking a neutral point of view makes no sense according to determinism. Further, there is no necessity, either theoretical or pragmatic, in the facts it postulates. The Hobbesian account of deliberation, however false it may be, is not impossible. There is no reason in the nature of the case why external and internal causes ought

---

23. Indeed, as I argue in chapter 2, I could not rationally accept it even in that case.
24. Farrer, *Freedom of the Will*, 126–32.

not to compel subjective reactions, regardless of the attitude we adopt toward the process of evoking them. Yet precisely what needs explaining is the apparent necessity of the attitude of agency for action, which follows straightaway on the assumption of free will.

To put it another way, the simplest, most natural and straightforward explanation of something's *appearing* to be such and such is that it *is* such and such. This is not irrefutable proof, but it does create an initial presumption in favor of that most natural hypothesis, one that can only be overcome by significant evidence to the contrary. If what I argue in the next chapter is correct, however, we need not fear that any such evidence will be discovered, since its discovery would undermine our confidence in the very cognitive faculties used to discover those putative facts. Thus, we need not fear that this presumption is at risk from the results of scientific research. Nor does the strength of this presumption rely in any way on our being able to explain or eliminate the mystery of free will, although I will argue in the third chapter of this book that there is a way we can coherently conceive free will.

OBJECTIONS AND REPLIES

If the foregoing is correct, there is no hope of reducing or eliminating the subjective point of view on action. Instead, human action, like consciousness itself, must always lie beyond the grasp of "the view from nowhere" as constituted by the perspective of natural science. As such, belief in free will seems to leave our view of the world permanently bifurcated, and one naturally wants to ask if anything untoward follows from this. For my part, I cannot see that it does.

That the world is largely deterministic and thus capable of exhaustive scientific explanation is not a problem for the proponent of free will, since only if the world is largely regular is free will even possible. A structureless world in which anything could and did happen would make knowledge of our actions impossible and hence much diminish the scope of free choice. The apparent uniqueness of free will in an otherwise deterministic world is a scandal and an anomaly only from the deterministic point of view; on the supposition that there is free will, it is what one would naturally expect.

Yet what are we to make of the actions of others? A determinist might contend that on this sort of reasoning, the same ought to hold of the actions of others, since unless individual human actions are predictable, the value of free choice would be greatly diminished. At the same time, of course, if individual human actions are predictable, then it is likely that individual human actions have causes and that there is no free will. Thus, if a basic condition for free will is met in the case of individual human actions, it appears to undermine, or at least circumscribe, that very possibility.

Fortunately, Farrer (among others) has shown how the predictability of individual human actions is, in fact, consistent with belief in the freedom of the will. Since we ourselves are agents, it is possible for us to interpret and understand the actions of others by reference to our own agency. All that is required for this sort of interpretation to be possible is that other agents be connatural to me, i.e., have roughly the same motivational structure as I do and thus a standard set of human responses to situations and circumstances. Given this, plus imagination sufficient to conceive oneself as exercising agency in someone else's situation, we can understand and predict the behavior of others without reliance on specific causes or causal theories of human behavior. As Farrer points out, some of the predictions we make, for example, that a party guest will entertain because of his witty and unpredictable behavior, are inconsistent with the supposition that they are made from an explicit knowledge of causes.

This does not exclude the possibility that we may sometimes be wrong about or mystified by what we ourselves or others do, or even that there is no legitimate role for causal explanation in explaining at least some human actions. There is nothing to prevent a happy bridegroom from going out and hanging himself on his wedding day, except that neither he nor anyone else can see any reason why he should. Yet if he does so, it is typically only then that we seek some sort of causal explanation for his extraordinary behavior. The psychologist may speculate that he acted under the aegis of a sudden, irresistible impulse and the police that he was murdered. Cases of this sort, otherwise opaque to reason, are comparatively rare; the determinist's insistence that this is the standard case seems implausible on the face of it.

There appears to be no significant advantage, let alone necessity, in adopting the external, or objective, point of view with regard to human action, whether in our own case or that of others. Indeed, it appears that little if anything is to be gained from doing so, no pressing theoretical demand requiring us to transcend our ordinary ways of understanding and speaking about human action. Indeed, the danger appears to lie in the other direction, since it does not appear that there is any way to make sense of our ordinary conception of ourselves if determinism is true, even as that self-conception informs our understanding of what we are doing when we do science and philosophy. While free will (like consciousness itself) may appear to be extremely mysterious because it stubbornly resists causal explanation by its very nature, we may well at this point be willing to rest content with that rather than deny what appears to be an obvious fact of experience.

What would overcome the experiential presumption in favor of free will? Nothing less, I think, than the establishment of a detailed and well-confirmed deterministic account of human action, one which not only provided an account of human behavior but which was also capable of explaining the process of rational thought, belief formation, discourse, and intellectual inquiry in a way that does not compromise the autonomy of reason and its truth-directedness. For reasons we will see, there is no prospect of any such thing succeeding, not simply as an empirical matter, but in the very nature of the case. Therefore, I think we may conclude that the presumption in favor of free will stands and is likely to stand regardless of the course of future scientific research.

Determinism and Scientific Realism

Of course, we can hardly expect that the determinist will let this go unchallenged. Indeed, most scientifically minded exponents of determinism have an explicit theoretical commitment to *scientific realism*, the view that successful scientific theories are objectively true about the external world.[25] Indeed, such philosophers are likely to hold that it is precisely because they accept scientific realism that they are determinists and that those who accept scientific realism and are not determinists simply have not exposed themselves to the relevant evidence.[26] Sometimes, it is suggested that such people are willfully irrational on this matter due to certain prescientific commitments they may have. Others, such as Saul Smilansky, argue that there are good evolutionary reasons why we should possess the illusion of free will.[27] Of course, if hard determinism is true,

---

25. See, e.g., Double, *Non-Reality of Free Will*, 7.
26. See, e.g., Honderich, *How Free Are You?*, 65–80.
27. Smilansky, "*Free Will*," in Kane, *Oxford Handbook*, 489–506.

there can be no such thing as *willful* irrationality—people believe what they have been caused to believe by forces beyond their control and can hardly be blamed for this. Only a rational being that has a choice about what to believe could be irrational in the normative sense that implies blameworthiness. Further, there are undoubtedly many people who have "exposed themselves" to the evidence that the determinist finds convincing but who are not themselves convinced. It would be question begging to claim that this is sufficient by itself to convict them of irrationality; after all, there are nonrational motives for belief in determinism, such as a prephilosophical commitment to atheism or a desire to avoid moral responsibility for one's actions that might be distorting one's take on the evidence. Further, if we are somehow genetically determined to believe that we have free will, one wonders how Smilansky and other determinists have managed to slip the chains of illusion. Apparently, this illusion can be overcome, since they themselves are living proof of this. No doubt, they would reply that they overcame it by exposing themselves to the scientific evidence for determinism, which ultimately convinced them of its truth and will convince anyone else who is not blinded by irrational attachments to outmoded notions of freedom, dignity, and the meaning of life that only free will can justify. I will discuss this challenge in chapter 2. At this point, I propose to deal with the classical difficulty for freedom concerning the will, a version of the interaction problem for substance dualism. Let us now go on to consider this in more detail.

2

Mind and Body

THE LIMITS OF THE SCIENTIFIC IMAGE

IN HIS FAMOUS PAPER, "Philosophy and the Scientific Picture of Man," Wilfrid Sellars contrasts two different ways of thinking about "man-in-the-world," which he calls the "manifest image" and the "scientific image," respectively.[1] The manifest image takes it that human beings and the objects of everyday experience are fundamentally real and apprehended pretheoretically in such a way that the statements we make about them are privileged. Every classical philosopher from Plato to G. E. Moore apparently endorses this position, including the ordinary language philosophers.[2] By contrast, those working within the tradition of modern scientific realism apply the apparent findings of natural science to our understanding of the human person, producing the scientific image according to which human beings are just another natural phenomenon, all of whose capacities and powers are ultimately explicable in the categories of physics and the other positive sciences.[3] Sellars notes that the juxtaposition of the manifest image, itself an articulation of what he calls the "original image" (which regarded all reality as imbued with personality), and the scientific image leads to conflict and cognitive dis-

---

1. Sellars, *Science, Perception, and Reality*, 1–40.

2. Ibid., 7–8.

3. Actually, Sellars is more modest than this, maintaining that *qualia*, intentions, and social facts are not reducible to physics or to any science reducible to physics; despite this, he apparently remains committed to the notion that everything that exists is physical. Those imbued with this Sellarsian vision, which is now an established dogma accepted without question or argument by many philosophers, have long since denied these limitations on the scientific image. If he were alive today, I suspect that Sellars would probably agree with them.

sonance. A similar conflict arises from the juxtaposition of the picture of material things derived from sense perception and that derived from physics captured in the image of Eddington's two tables. In the case of Eddington's table, most of us are willing to say that the physical account of the table is the truth about the matter and that the manifest image of the table derived from sense experience must be accommodated to that fact by being treated as merely (at most) an appearance of that table in consciousness. In Sellars's time, however, there was still significant resistance to the idea that we could replace the manifest image of the human person with the scientific image ultimately based in neurophysiology. There is little doubt about this now, so I am somewhat embarrassed to have to oppose the weighty consensus in its behalf. However, I will oppose it with what seem to me weighty and conclusive, if only philosophical, arguments.[4]

Let us focus on something that Sellars does believe will prove reducible without remainder to psychophysical states of the brain, what he calls "conceptual thinking."[5] Although Sellars does not define this term, or even illustrate it, it seems clear enough that by conceptual thinking he means what we ordinarily mean by the word "thinking" as we use it in everyday speech. In this sense, "thinking" is thinking *about* something, an activity distinct from the contemplation of mental images, involving concepts functioning as signs of external objects and expressible in the language of theoretical inquiry, such as philosophy and natural science. Sellars believes that conceptual thinking is in principle reducible to and expressible within the constraints of the scientific image, because unlike *qualia*, which are incapable of being described or experienced without reference to their role as the appearances of things, conceptual thinking

---

4. I have stated these arguments in a much more rigorous way, elsewhere in an unpublished manuscript. There I argue that the metaphysical system called "philosophy as continuous with science" is epistemically self-refuting, by which I mean that, given the presuppositions and apparent implications of that metaphysical system, we can never have any reason to believe that it is true. As such, if we take this metaphysical system seriously, it undermines any reasons we might have for believing it and, indeed, the whole process of believing based on reasons. The argument given here is a sketch of that larger argument given in the aforementioned text. For another version of this argument, see Duncan, "Strange Case," posted to *PhilPapers*.

5. Sellars, *Science, Perception, and Reality*, 32–35. Sellars appears to be outlining an early version of functionalism, which is (roughly) the view that thought/consciousness is simply whatever it is that mediates input (in the form of sense-data) and output (in the form of externally observable behavior). According to this view, there is no reason in principle why thought could not turn out to be identical with some sort of brain process.

has no such intrinsic "aspectual" character.[6] Even if our explicit thinking episodes are introspectible and have a characteristic phenomenology, this plays no essential role in that activity itself, so that there is no reason to suppose (resist?) the idea that thoughts and thinking are simply identical with states and processes occurring in the brain.

Although Sellars does not discuss this point, one supposes that he regards brain states and processes as embedded in, or constituted by, sequences of physical events related solely by efficient causal connections, so that each such state or each stage in the process can (*in principle*) be completely accounted for by the operation of the laws of physics. In that case, conceptual thinking is constituted by, and reducible without remainder to, some purely physical process occurring in the brain, produced and dictated solely by antecedent physical states and relations of efficient causal dependence between those states. However, this picture, itself a direct result of the preference for the scientific image as applied to the activity of conceptual thinking, leads immediately to a problem. If conceptual thinking is, in fact, constituted in the way that Sellars suggests (and many others today believe it to be), we have no reason to believe that any such state or process would ever lead us to the discovery of theoretical truth. While it is not impossible that a purely physical process with purely physical antecedents might *accidentally* embody, say, a valid and sound deductive argument, or proper scientific reasoning, it could not do so *intrinsically*. That is because the connections between concepts and their objects, propositions and their contents, premises and conclusions, and hypotheses and the evidence that confirms or disconfirms them are *logical* rather than *causal*. As such, no series of physical events connected merely by relations of efficient causality can constitute a valid inference or proper scientific reasoning even if we imagine that it could somehow physically *realize* such things.[7] Since there is no intrinsic connection between any

---

6. See Searle, *Rediscovery of the Mind*, 78–82, 155–57, on this use of "aspectual."

7. Ibid., 197–226. Searle appears to hold such a view. That does not mean that he would have any sympathy with the view advanced here, as he clearly does not. Incidentally, it would make no difference to the argument I am making here, if, rightly rejecting physicalist reductionism, one were to postulate (as does Honderich at one point) that mental events somehow piggyback on these externally related physical events in the brain. Mental events, so understood, exercise no causal powers of their own and, as Honderich himself admits, could not do so in any case. See Honderich, *How Free Are You?*, chapters 3–5. Such states and their properties could play no role at all in explaining any of my beliefs, even if they, in fact, possess them, nor could we even know that this was so. See Duncan, "Consequences of Neurophysiological

sort of causal physical process and such things as deductive validity or proper scientific reasoning, that any such process would realize things such as these can only be purely accidental features of those processes. Thus, insofar as conceptual thinking is constituted by nothing but (or wholly dependent upon) externally related, efficient causal physical states and processes, we have no reason to believe that they constitute valid and sound deductive arguments or proper scientific reasoning. Given this, we can have no reason to believe that any process constituted in that way does, *in fact,* constitute an example of conceptual thinking as we ordinarily understand it in accordance with the manifest image.

From that ordinary point of view, conceptual thinking involves concepts, propositions, and logical relations between concepts (such as analyticity), propositions (such as implication) and events (such as C being necessary and sufficient for the occurrence of E). Further, such relations are *intrinsic* to conceptual thinking: such relations essentially constitute arguments, explanations, and so on. In turn, theoretical constructs, like the manifest and scientific images of reality, are essentially constituted by concepts and their meanings, arguments and explanations, such as those that compose philosophy and natural science. Only if we can rely on our abilities to grasp the meanings of concepts and use them to form true propositions, to evaluate the soundness of arguments, to arrive at well-confirmed explanations, and so on, can we have any reason to suppose that we have any hold at all on theoretical truth. This, after all, is the *goal* of conceptual thinking and the reason we engage in it in the first place.

Further and most importantly, unless we can engage in conceptual thinking prior to and independently of our knowledge of the existence and functioning of the brain, it will be impossible for us even to discover the materials necessary to construct and confirm the scientific image itself. In and of itself, we can have no purely physical reason for supposing that any brain process constitutes a sound deductive argument or correct explanation of anything, even of how the brain itself works. Indeed, we know the brain and its processes only by using conceptual thinking and have no reason to believe that the brain itself can even be an object of knowledge unless conceptual thinking is *somehow truth-connected* independently of its having been physically realized in some sort of brain process. We can only know that this is the case if conceptual thinking is

---

Determinism," posted to *PhilPapers*, and the rest of this chapter.

autonomous of the operation of the brain and functions for us as it does according to the manifest image of human reasoning captured in traditional formal logic, philosophy, and scientific method. All of these are species of conceptual thinking and thus products of the manifest image of reality and the human person, not of the scientific image embodied in physicalism. Like philosophy itself, all science, including neuroscience, is a species of conceptual thinking and is incomprehensible apart from the manifest image in which the notion of conceptual thinking finds its natural home. Indeed, we can trust neuroscience itself only if we can justify its claims as true, and this is not possible apart from the use of conceptual thinking, because the *very notions* of conceptual thinking, of linguistic meaning, rational discourse, theoretical inquiry, and of philosophy and natural science considered as forms of that activity are themselves elements of the manifest image. Natural science, then, is supposed to be an example of the very sort of conceptual thinking that this advanced neuroscience is intended to supersede.

Therefore, unless conceptual thinking as construed in accordance with the manifest image is sound (and thus in no need of being superseded), such an account cannot be established to begin with. Nor can such a theory wholly contradict or undermine conceptual thinking as understood according to the manifest image without to that extent undermining any reason we might have for believing it. It will be credible only to the extent that it conforms to what rationality requires from the point of view of the manifest image; to that extent, then, it will be unable by that very fact to supersede it. Given that such an account could only be established using the methods of natural science, there is no prospect of replacing conceptual thinking with some sort of advanced neurophysiological account of cognition.

The upshot is this: Rational belief and the means for its acquisition belong to the manifest image. This means that in order for us to have any reason for believing anything *at all*, the sort of reasoning that constitutes theoretical inquiry and which has conceptual thinking/rational discourse as its medium must be *intrinsically*, and not merely *accidentally*, truth-directed. This, in turn, will be possible only if the cognitive faculties by means of which we carry on this theoretical activity are *autonomous* of the operation of any process going on in the brain, in two senses. First, it cannot be constituted by or identical with any *merely* physical set of states or processes occurring in the brain, because we have no reason to suppose that any such process, considered *as such*, could realize conceptual thinking/rational discourse or theoretical inquiry in any but an accidental way.[8] This is because no such state or process considered as such can be intrinsically truth-connected in the way required to constitute successful theoretical inquiry. Second, the standards for evaluation of the products of that inquiry must be *knowable* independent of any of the substantive results of natural scientific inquiry, including neurophysiology and anything we know about the brain. Otherwise, we will not be able to acquire the necessary knowledge about the brain required to reduce intellectual inquiry to its operation. In other words, our *access* to the elements of conceptual thinking has to be independent of our scientific knowledge, inasmuch as scientific knowledge is itself the product of conceptual thinking, rational discourse, and theoretical inquiry. As such, the priority of the manifest image over the scientific image remains intact; we cannot abandon the one for the other, especially in the realm of conceptual thinking, without abandoning rationality altogether.

Almost certainly, someone will object that, even if everything I have said is true, the consequences of this are hardly as dire as I have made them out. Even if my rational thought processes are nothing but electrochemical states and processes occurring in my brain, this does not rule out the possibility that (however accidentally) they do track truth. In that case, we ought to be able to judge that this is the case by examining our thought processes critically in order to determine whether they constitute sound reasoning or well-confirmed explanations of phenomena. To make this suggestion, however, is to fail to recognize the seriousness of the problem here. If our conceptual thinking is nothing but an electrochemical process occurring in our brains, or something wholly dependent on such a process, then so are our judgments concerning the validity of arguments and the degree to which scientific evidence confirms potential explanations of phenomena. They are at best electrochemical states of such a process. As such, they are themselves at best accidentally

---

8. Of course, we can program a computer to do mathematical calculations, play chess, create truth tables, and so on. However, to the extent that we can assign any activity to the computer itself, all the computer does is "crunch numbers." The relation between the activity of "playing chess" (which the computer engages in at best by analogy) and the operation of the machine realizes that activity in a purely accidental fashion. The explanation of its ability to play chess has quite another source, in the intentional activity of the team that programmed the computer to do so. In our own case, however, we can have no reason to believe that we have been "programmed" to know the way the world is, *unless* we are theists. See below.

rational and thus no more trustworthy than the original judgments they are intended to validate or criticize. So the notion that we might be able to examine our thought processes in order to determine which of them are accidentally rational and which are not simply dissipates.[9] Unless human reason is *autonomous* in making such judgments and capable of evaluating the validity of arguments and the degree to which evidence confirms explanations on logical and methodological grounds alone, we can have no reason to believe that we even possess the ability to do so, let alone trust the results of our exercises of that putative ability. Thus, if conceptual thinking is nothing but an electrochemical process occurring in the brain, our judgment to this effect, even if based on a review of what we take to be the relevant evidence, will provide no reason for us to believe that it is true or likely to be true.

The standard and most common response to this claim is to retreat to an externalist standard for rational belief as a way of avoiding the implicit internalism of the foregoing account of conceptual thinking. According to this alternative picture, it is sufficient for our beliefs to be true, and thus for them to be rational beliefs, that we be *caused to believe them in the right way*, i.e., by reliable cognitive faculties that produce a high percentage of true beliefs. On this picture, one does not need to *know* that one possesses such faculties or *which* of those beliefs are actually true; it simply has to be a *fact* that they are produced in this way in order for those beliefs to be rational and count as knowledge for us. Of course, on the supposition that conceptual thought is nothing but an electrochemical process occurring in our brains, we have no reason whatsoever to suppose that we do, in fact, possess such faculties or that their deliverances are likely to be true—at least to the extent that we can sensibly judge this to be the case. Given that any such process is at best accidentally rational, so far as we know, physical processes have no natural tendency to track truth or realize true beliefs about reality of the sort that are the subject matter of conceptual thinking and theoretical inquiry. Nor will it do for the externalist to appeal to coherence, consistency, or the apparent stability of our beliefs for two reasons: First, to do so is at least tacitly to admit that the externalist picture needs to be

---

9. Indeed, since any such proposal requires that we have independent, introspective access to our thought processes, it is already committed to the idea of the autonomy of reason and thus to the rejection of the scientific image in this context. On this point, see Duncan, "Could Introspection Be Unreliable?" and "Can I Know What I Am Thinking?," both posted to *PhilPapers*.

justified or confirmed by proof, or evidence, in some way. In that case, it surrenders to its internalist rival and thus represents no gain over it. Second, if the externalist sticks to his guns and eschews the internalist standard of epistemic justification, then we will have reason to trust our judgments as to the coherence, etc., of our beliefs only if we have reason to believe that reliable cognitive faculties produced them, which is the very point at issue. So, then, such an appeal is circular.

At this point, the externalist will undoubtedly appeal to evolution as a mechanism capable of providing a plausible explanation for our possession of reliable cognitive faculties. The claim will be that, since false belief is generally maladaptive, we can expect that evolution would have selected for reliable cognitive faculties. The proposal has its greatest plausibility with regard to the faculties responsible for *basic* beliefs, i.e., spontaneously occurring beliefs about local states of affairs (such as sense-perception memory and casual induction), since these are directly related to survival and differential reproduction. With regard to *theoretical* beliefs that are the product of conceptual thinking, however, this proposal has no plausibility whatsoever. We have no reason at all for supposing that evolution would endow us with cognitive faculties capable of discovering theoretical truths about the nature of reality, i.e., cognitive faculties directed on truth as such without any direct reference to survival or differential reproduction. Given this, there is no reason whatsoever for believing that evolution is true, since it is itself a product of the operation of those faculties and thus no more sound than they are reliable. At any rate, such an appeal is viciously circular in the same way that, on the standard interpretation, Descartes' proof of the external world is taken to be—wrongly in my view.[10] I cannot use my cognitive faculties to justify my belief in the theory of evolution and then use evolution to justify my belief in the reliability of the cognitive faculties by means of which I arrived at my belief in evolution. This is either to use evolution to justify itself or to beg the question with regard to the reliability of my cognitive faculties. If we could establish either of these claims independently of the other, we could plausibly argue from one to the other; as it is, however, this whole approach simply leaves us spinning our wheels, regardless of whether the theory of evolution is true.[11]

10. Duncan, *Proof,* chapter 1.

11. My claim, then, is not that the theory of evolution is false, but rather that it cannot be used in the manner envisaged here, i.e., to justify the claim that we possess

We have found no alternative, then, to admitting that conceptual thought is the product of an *autonomous reason*, constituted by cognitive faculties whose operations are *intrinsically* rational (i.e., truth directed and, when used properly, capable of tracking theoretical truth about reality) and governed by and to be evaluated in terms of logical rather than neurophysiological standards of adequacy. Given this, it is not possible that conceptual thinking could be *simply* identical with, reducible without remainder to, or proved in the last analysis to be *nothing but* physical states or processes occurring in the brain, since these could be at best accidentally rational and exhaustively explicable in terms of the operation of efficient causes that are themselves wholly physical. In the end, we must admit that, whatever conceptual thinking consists in, it is not simply an electrochemical, neurophysiological brain process, on pain of eliminating any possibility of having any rational beliefs about anything, including the functioning of the brain.[12] The limits of the scientific image, then, are to be found in the very possibility of science as a branch of theoretical inquiry. The discovery of those limits fully vindicates the priority of the manifest image over the scientific image, at least where what Sellars calls "conceptual thinking" is concerned. Rather than it being necessary to adjust the manifest image to the scientific image in this context, it is the other way around—the scientific image needs to be accommodated to the manifest image. Let us now briefly consider how to do this.

THE PRIMA FACIE CASE FOR DUALISM

Elsewhere I have argued that there is an experiential presumption in favor of dualism based on our ordinary, everyday experience of ourselves as both rational, self-conscious subjects and as apparently embodied and that the failure of alternative theories leaves this presumption undefeated.[13] I have also argued in a different context that the epistemically self-refuting character of physicalism about mind shows that substance dualism of the Cartesian sort is a necessary presupposition for the possibility of rational discourse and thus eminently rational for us to believe

---

reliable cognitive faculties. The theory of evolution will only be acceptable if it can be justified by cognitive faculties whose reliability can be proved apart from that theory.

12. Nor could this be the case if "mental events" (which, in any case, do not exist) were nomically dependent on nonrational, purely physical brain events and "connected" to one another solely through external, efficient causal relations. Duncan, "Thinking?," posted to *PhilPapers*.

13. Duncan, "Dualism and Neuroscience," posted to *PhilPapers*.

for that reason alone.[14] Here I want to build on the argument of the previous section and suggest that we have the same reasons for rejecting the thesis that intentional mental states are identical with brain states as we have for rejecting the thesis that, in sense perception, we are immediately aware of external objects. Just as on the traditional account of sense perception, "sense-data" are subjective, mind-dependent, mental contents that exist independently of the external objects that they putatively represent, so too are mental contents, considered as such, ontologically distinct from the brain states and processes that may be in some way associated with their occurrence. In making this argument, I will be stressing the parallelism between the traditional argument for representational realism and the relation between mental contents as such and their supposed "realization" in brain states and processes. The points I will make are hardly original; however, I believe that the strategy of my argument is slightly different from those of other arguments lurking in the same neighborhood. Let us take the argument in stages.

The Essential Immediacy of Awareness

As I have argued elsewhere, consciousness is awareness-as-such, the fundamental activity by means of which we apprehend sensations, feelings, qualia, and our own mental states and acts (in some cases at least) as the operation of the substantial self.[15] Through the power of introspection and voluntary control of our attention, we can progressively shift foreground and background in our intentional field, thus bringing into clear and distinct centrality features of our conscious lives that are generally peripheral to, or in the background of, our ordinary conscious experience. Mystical experience aside, awareness is always "awareness of," i.e., focused on a *content* that constitutes a phenomenologically distinct mode of awareness. Some contents, such as mental images, are intentional and have putative extramental objects that they make present to us in consciousness. Others, such as pains and tickles, are non-intentional and lack objects. However, when apprehended introspectively, every mental content of whatever sort is also an object of awareness in its own right. That we are aware of such things as pains and tickles, mental images, mental states and acts as operations of the self, etc., I take to be

---

14. See "Is Neuroscience Possible?," posted to *PhilPapers* for part of that argument.
15. Duncan, *Proof*, chapter 4, especially 87–89.

an undeniable fact of immediate experience, known with more immediate certainty than *any* fact of natural science.[16]

However, in order for awareness to be possible at all, the act of apprehension must terminate in some object apprehended *directly* or *immediately*, without further ado or without intermediary—for unless I apprehend something directly, i.e., without apprehending something else first, apprehension can never terminate *at all*. If I can only apprehend something by apprehending something else first, then nothing can be apprehended. Nevertheless, as we clearly know from the Cartesian *Cogito*, I am a conscious subject and do, in fact, apprehend the contents of my own consciousness.[17] It remains, then, that since the spontaneously arising contents of consciousness inhabiting my intentional field of awareness are the terminus of my act of awareness, they are also that of which I am directly and immediately aware. We know nothing with greater certainty than this and, apart from this, can know nothing; as such, it makes perfect sense to begin our search for knowledge from this basis.[18] However, this obviously raises the next question: In being aware of the contents of consciousness, what is that of which we are aware?

The Subjectivity of the Mental

It is an evident fact of experience that all conscious experience is subjective in the sense that it is something that happens in and to an individual conscious subject. Even when people share "the same experience," each does so by means of his or her own particular stream of consciousness and from a unique and unrepeatable perspective relative to all other individual consciousnesses. Further, each person's stream of consciousness is sealed off from every other and incommunicable in its character as *lived* experience—this is the core truth underlying the traditional notion of "privileged access." Even if the self is a "social construct" in some sense, this at most means that our discrete, individual perspective on reality is in

---

16. See below and Duncan, "Could Introspection Be Unreliable?," posted to *PhilPapers*. Indeed, it ought to be obvious on very little reflection that any scientific fact that I claim to know is known to me only through its being an immediate object of thought occurring in my consciousness. If this were not so, we could know nothing at all.

17. Duncan, *Proof*, chapter 4, especially 73–76.

18. Of course, if we fail to find knowledge in so doing, then perhaps we ought to abandon the quest for knowledge and settle for something else, such as Dewey's "warranted assertibility," or just embrace skepticism outright. However, I have argued that there is no need for this; ibid., especially chapter 9.

some way influenced by cultural norms and expectations, not that there is literally some sort of ownerless "group mind," or consciousness, (like the Hegelian Absolute) in which we all somehow participate.[19] The Cartesian self as *res cogitans*, as a thinking thing considered separately from what it thinks about, is something whose existence is known by us with extrinsic certainty; not even the Evil Genius could deceive us about this.

Furthermore, in introspection we discover that it is possible for us to alter and exercise a limited measure of control over the contents of consciousness. While we cannot control what we will see, hear, etc., during our waking experience, we do possess the power to voluntarily attend to some things rather than others, alter foreground and background in consciousness, and even in some cases control the order in which our experiences occur in time.[20] In all these respects, then, consciousness is subjective and mind dependent, even in those cases where I make no effort to "control" the course or character of my awareness of things. Yet what about the intentional contents of our subjective awareness? Are they subjective as well, or constituted objectively, independently of consciousness and simply somehow in relation to consciousness? This, of course, is the fundamental problem of the philosophy of perception. Let me tell the oft-told tale again, for it is relevant to the point I am trying to make here. I will be brief, however, due to the familiarity of that story to all of us.

The Case for Representationalism

Sense perception is the most familiar fact in the world and structures nearly all of our everyday experience. So much is this the case that we rarely advert to sense experience itself at all; instead, our attention is focused outward onto the intentional objects made present to us by sense experience constituting a realm of external objects existing independently of consciousness. More than this, sense perception proves, in the main, to be extremely reliable in practice; very few of the spontaneous

---

19. Mead, *Selected Writings*, 134–49. Of course, I hold no brief for such a view, but it is not my purpose here to criticize it. At any rate, Mead, for one, was clearly aware of the distinction to be made between the "self" (which, under idealist influence, he regarded as a social construct) and the "ego," the individual conscious subject in which the self is "housed."

20. Recall Kant's example (*Kritik*, B234–5/A190) of the man standing outside his apartment house, whose experience of the building's various parts, though successive in time, is ordered in a thoroughly subjective manner that does not reflect any objective order in the events.

judgments it leads us to form need to be revised in light of subsequent experience. It is therefore the most natural thing in the world for us to take sense experience at face value and to suppose that it is a largely accurate, literal description of the external world. The view known as "direct," or "naïve," realism is the theoretical articulation, within the philosophy of perception, of this common-sense view. Although it has defenders even in contemporary philosophy, the basic problem for direct realism becomes clear once we seriously begin to consider the relation of the subject and object in the perceptual act.[21] In order for direct realism to be true, the external object itself must also be the intentional content of the perceptual act—the perceptual act must terminate in the apprehension of the surface of the external object perceived. The Stoics, Augustine, and some of the Arab thinkers endorsed the *extramission* theory, first suggested by Euclid, to explain how this might be possible.[22] According to this theory, rays emanating from the eye make direct contact with the surface of the external object itself so that perception actually takes place in the external world on the surface of the objects themselves.[23]

This theory was never very plausible, but its insufficiency became evident within the context provided by the New Science, which combines scientific realism with the ontology of Galilean physicalism, as I have described elsewhere.[24] If the New Science is literally true, then direct realism has to be false on two grounds. First, given external objects are nothing more than what mathematical physics takes them to be—temporary aggregates of material particles interacting in accordance with the basic laws of motion—it is clear that none of the properties that we apprehend in ordinary sense perception literally inhere in those bodies. At best, our qualia correspond to dispositional properties possessed by external objects in virtue of their physical microstructure by means of which they causally produce perceptual qualia in us.[25] Second,

21. See, e.g., Smith, *Problem of Perception*, and Huemer, *Skepticism and the Veil*, both of whom defend direct realism, a view I myself once entertained.

22. Lindberg, *Theories of Vision*, chapters 1–3. Aristotle may have held this theory as well, at least at one point; see, e.g., *De Caelo*, 290a1, 14–25 and Lindberg, ibid., 217–18, n. 39.

23. Ibid., 6–26. Actually, this is something of a simplification; extramission theorists tend to claim that the visual ray is then reflected back to the eye, thus producing the visual image in the eye.

24. Duncan, *Proof*, chapter 1.

25. Locke, *Essay*, II, VIII, 1–10. This is Locke's all too brief account of the "second-

the physical mechanism of perception, involving various forms of wave radiation being absorbed and reflected by bodies, striking our sense organs and stimulating our nerves, etc., is clearly inconsistent with the extramission theory. In the face of this, those committed to the New Physics automatically moved toward the mainstream philosophical view about perception, the view now known as "representationalism" or "representational realism."

Representationalism asserts that the intentional object of the perceptual act and the intentional content by means of which we apprehend it are both ontologically distinct from one another and possess no properties unambiguously in common. According to representationalism, the intentional contents by means of which our thoughts are directed to external objects are *wholly* subjective and mind dependent, related to their intentional object only by a productive, external causal process, the perceptual mechanism I adumbrated in the last paragraph. Further, none of the properties that we experience external objects to have in sense perception exist in those objects as we experience them. Redness as consciously experienced is a particular sort of *quale* associated with fire engines, stop lights, and socialist banners. Redness as it exists in external bodies is merely a dispositional property to absorb all but the wavelengths of light belonging to the red spectrum as measured by scientific instruments and to reflect the waves that it does not absorb. According to this view, if there were no perceivers, there would be no such thing as redness as we experience it in sense perception, whereas objects would still absorb and reflect light waves regardless of that fact, hence would still be colored in the scientific sense of that term. Having banished these properties *as experienced* from the external world, there was no choice but to postulate *somewhere else* for them to be, namely, an immaterial mind or soul, the essence of which is to be conscious. This mind or soul becomes the repository for mental contents of all sorts, intentional and non-intentional, and the last outpost of spirit in the created world.

The epistemological problems generated by this picture are massive and well known; I have discussed them elsewhere.[26] The inability of early modern philosophers (whether rationalist or empiricist) to solve these

---

ary qualities."

26. Duncan, *Proof*, 4-8. However, I go on to argue that we can complete the Cartesian project of providing a foundation for the reliability of our cognitive faculties in the veracity of God. This solves the otherwise insoluble epistemological problems generated by representational realism.

problems spawned the skepticism of Hume and the dogmatism of the Scottish School of Common Sense. Kant made a new beginning with his *Critique of Pure Reason,* but this, in turn, spawned German idealism, from which philosophers made a decisive break in the early twentieth century. However, the problem of fitting consciousness into the scientific worldview remained into the twentieth century; the various forms of materialism, behaviorism, functionalism, and so on were its response to these problems. It is to that part of the problem that we now turn.

The Futility of Materialism

Representationalism treats mental contents and their objects as entities of utterly diverse orders and natures. Idealists and phenomenalists, uncomfortable with this dualism, attempted to overcome the bifurcation of the world into mind and matter either by eliminating the external world or reducing its objects to consciousness itself and its elements. The first form of idealism (reminiscent of Berkeley) denies that any external world exists at all. The second form of idealism embraces an all-encompassing monism in which all of reality is absorbed into a single Absolute mind, à la Hegel, while phenomenalists attempt to show that the world is merely a construction out of sense-data conceived of as self-existing atoms of thought, à la Hartley, Hume, and the logical positivists. Contemporary monistic materialism (often called "physicalism about mind") follows suit, simply replicating from its own monist perspective the same positions occupied by the idealists.

One view, eliminative materialism, simply denies that there is any such thing as mind at all, along with consciousness, lived experience, mental contents, qualia, or anything at all describable using "mental" predicates. The other, reductive materialism, maintains that what we call "mind" is identical with (meaning *nothing but* or *reducible without remainder*) to the brain considered as a merely physical system exhaustively describable in wholly objective, nonmental terms. According to the first view, there is no such thing as my (or anyone else's) experience of redness consisting in my immediate awareness of a red quale, since there is no such thing as awareness or qualia to begin with. According to the second view, one's awareness of a red quale really occurs and exists; it is just that it turns out, on analysis, to be *reductively identical* with, i.e., *nothing but,* a purely physical process occurring in the brain that possesses only physical properties. Neither of these views is at all plausible, but the overwhelming number of philosophers and scientists remain stubbornly, dogmatically committed to some version of physicalism about mind, so much so that they have largely ceased even to argue for it, and, instead, simply take it for granted that it is true.

The first view, eliminative materialism, is clearly false for two obvious reasons. First, we simply know, *immediately* and with *extrinsic certainty*, that we are self-conscious, rational subjects: *cogito ergo sum*. Since we could not be self-conscious, rational subjects if eliminative materialism were true, and we are not even *possibly* wrong about that fact, eliminative materialism must be false—Q.E.D. Second, eliminative materialists base their denial of consciousness on the findings of science; like Laplace, they have no need for that hypothesis, which they regard as an outmoded theory that modern science supersedes. Yet on the assumption that eliminative materialism is true, it is difficult to comprehend how science itself, conceived of as rational, theoretical inquiry, can even exist. If there is no consciousness, there are no phenomena, hence nothing for science to be about. If there are no self-conscious rational subjects, where is the wonder that evokes curiosity about the phenomena and leads to rational inquiry? How is it possible for us to construct theories, test them in experience, and proclaim them true, or at least warranted, since all of these are the deliberate, self-conscious actions of scientists and philosophers attempting to understand the way the world works? The notion that science somehow does itself without the need for self-conscious, rational inquirers makes its existence utterly ungrounded and mysterious.

Perhaps an inchoate realization of the absurdity of eliminative materialism explains why the view has had and continues to have few adherents, despite its being the only consistent view that a materialist can take. Reductive materialists do not deny that we are conscious or that conscious experience occurs. However, in numerous ways too diverse to detail here, each school of reductive materialism attempts to show that the mind is nothing but the brain and that mental contents are nothing but physical states of the brain or physical properties of those states. This remains the mainstream position despite the fact that the actual reduction of the mental to the physical remains as incomplete and elusive as ever, never getting beyond an ever more detailed set of correlations between mental states/properties and brain states/properties. I will now go on to characterize the fundamental absurdity in the reductive materialist project, one that has been articulated in various ways but none, I think, in a fully conclusive form.[27]

Let me first state the argument in its simplest form and then expand on it by considering each of its premises in turn:

I am immediately aware of the contents of my intentional field of consciousness.

If the contents of my intentional field of consciousness were nothing but my brain states and their properties, then I would be immediately aware of my brain states and their properties as such.[28]

I am not (normally) aware in any way of my brain states or their properties—they are not the contents of my mental states or acts.[29]

Therefore, it is not the case that the contents of my intentional field of consciousness are nothing but my brain states and their properties.

I argued earlier that, in order to be conscious at all, it is necessary that my awareness terminate in an object that it immediately apprehends as such and that it is the contents of our intentional field of consciousness that are those objects. If what the New Science teaches is correct, those contents cannot be the literal surfaces of external objects. Instead, along with Galileo and Descartes, we are forced to admit that *from that perspective*, the immediate objects of apprehension can only be *ideas*, mental contents that are ontologically distinct from the intentional ob-

---

27. Nagel, *View from Nowhere*, 165–180; *Last Word*, 32–46; and Searle, *Rediscovery*.

28. By "as such" here, I mean that I would directly and immediately apprehend them in conscious experience, from the private, subjective, first-person point of view, as nothing but congeries of physical entities possessing only physical properties. I would have to apprehend my thoughts not as thoughts but instead as a collection of atomic and subatomic particles, possessing only mass, spin, charge, direction, etc., subject to various forces (gravitation, the "weak force," etc.) and interacting with each other in accordance with the laws of motion. That I *never* actually apprehend any of my mental contents in this way, I take to be simple empirical fact and that as sufficient reason to suppose that I could never do so even in principle. There may be other senses of "as such" in which I could be said to apprehend my brain states as such, but these senses are not relevant to the argument I am making here.

29. This does not exclude the possibility that they might be *objects*, i.e., theoretical entities postulated as part of a theoretical construct intended to model and explain the phenomena we apprehend. However, I will endorse this notion only in a very limited version.

jects they represent to us and by which they are presumably caused.[30] In fact, I am never *immediately* aware of any external, material object or its properties. Instead, my knowledge of such objects is always mediated by a theoretical construct or theory that postulates such objects in order to explain the order and connection among my ideas, which evidently do not come from me.[31] In this regard, then, it is worth noting the obvious fact that *the brain, its processes, states, and properties are all external, material things and, as such, bid fair to be something that* **transcends consciousness**. Even if I were to cut my own head open and use a mirror to observe a certain part of my brain where my perceptual experience of my own brain was somehow supposed to be "taking place," I would decidedly not be perceptually aware of that experience itself.[32] Instead, I would simply be having a perceptual experience of a bit of brain tissue where certain electrochemical changes caused by light waves bouncing off the surface of my brain and redirected by the mirror were occurring. In any event, it could hardly be said that in being aware of my perceptual state in that way that I was immediately aware of some state of my brain; there is too much intervening causal machinery to make this claim plausible.

Since I am immediately aware of my mental processes, states, and properties, I am capable of exhaustively describing them when I clearly and distinctly perceive them. I simply "read them off" from my stream of consciousness and need neither theory nor inference in order to characterize them—natural language itself is enough to make this possible. Similarly, if I were immediately aware of my brain processes, states, and their properties, I would have no need of science in order to know what they are or how they function. In fact, however, my knowledge of the brain, its processes, states, and properties is all entirely indirect and based on theoretical inquiry: observation, inference, and experiment. It

---

30. That is to say, we are forced to this conclusion if what natural science tells us is the only consideration that we need to take into account here. Since this is the view of my materialist opponents, we will accept that claim in this context for the sake of the argument. In fact, however, I believe that this view is false, though not in a way that affects the point I am making here.

31. Of course, Kant and the constructivists would not agree. However, my materialist opponents are all scientific realists and so are generally opposed to this sort of view. At any rate, I have no space to take this up here.

32. Hook, *Determinism and Freedom*, 145–61. *Contra* the contention of Stephen Pepper in a famous thought experiment.

follows, then, that I am not immediately aware of my brain processes, their states, or properties and that whatever it is that I am immediately aware of is other than those things. It thus makes no sense to say that my mental contents are nothing but brain processes, brain states, or their properties.

There are other, less radical ways of attempting to characterize the "identity" relation between mind and brain. However, the foregoing should be enough to dispel the straightforward materialist position of concern to us here. Given that we have incorrigible evidence for the existence of mind and no reason to suppose that the mind is identical with the brain, we are surely justified in accepting the *prima facie* evidence on behalf of dualism. Materialists, however, will insist that we are not yet out of the woods, given the notorious *interaction problem* for dualism. We now turn to this issue, with which we will complete this chapter.

MIND AS PER SE SUSTAINING CAUSE OF BODILY STATES AND PROCESSES

Since the advent of the New Science, our conception of causation has been largely identical to the notion of efficient causation as described above. The mind/body problem as contemporary philosophers have discussed it, especially where dualist interactionism is concerned, has long been predicated on this conception of causation and of causal influence. In turn, this conception has largely shaped the debate about free will as well; we are told, for example, that the very notion of human agency, its expression in acts of volition, and enactment of volitions in bodily behavior are conceptually incoherent and physically impossible. Although these claims can be challenged, it remains that the view known as "hard libertarianism" about free will is at a decided disadvantage so long as our modern conception of efficient causation remains the only model for understanding causal influence. In my opinion, the mental cramp induced by this limited point of view must first be overcome before dualist interactionism and free will understood as involving liberty of indifference can be given a just hearing.

But where is such an alternative to be found? Despite the attractions of quantum indeterminism in physics, for the standard reasons I am not hopeful of finding much help or direct aid in providing the needed alternative from that source.[33] However, within the theistic tradition in philosophical theology, another conception of causal influence has been offered under the name of *divine conservation*. According to this idea, God directly causes all things other than himself to come into existence as the consequence of his act of Creation *ex nihilo* accomplished through an immediate act of willing (*fiat*); this, however, is not the full extent of God's creative activity. Since all things other than God have been created by him out of nothing (i.e., nothing preexisting independently of God's creative act), they have no power to remain in existence on their own. As such, it is required that God wills to sustain them in existence by *prolonging* that original act of Creation in time for as long as creatures continue to exist. In this way, God acts as the *causa in esse* (cause of being) of all created things, which has two aspects. First, there is the initial act of Creation, in which an act of divine agency exercised by the divine will conferred existence on things that otherwise would not exist. Second, there is the *continuous creation* of those things consisting in the prolongation of the initial act of Creation in time by means of which the *persistence* or *continuous* existence of those things is accomplished. What we nowadays call "causes" or "efficient causes," by contrast, are merely *causae in fieri* (causes of becoming) which presuppose both the initial and continued existence of that in which they produce mere changes of state or change of properties.[34]

Let me emphasize that a thing's causa in esse acts in it by sustaining its existence/persistence, not by endowing it with any particular set of observable properties or states. As I have characterized this elsewhere, a thing's causa in esse, more commonly known as its "per se," or "sustaining cause," accounts for its substantial unity, i.e., for the unity of existence-as-activity and limiting essence or nature in each individual existing thing other than God himself, in whom alone essence and existence are identical.[35] The various properties and states of creatures will be the consequence either of its essence (in the case of those properties

---

33. However, some materialists, such as Searle and Kane, have thought that perhaps something along these lines might work. I am not persuaded.

34. Suarez, *On Efficient Causality*, 281–82. Even in this third case, it has generally been thought that a further aspect of divine causality—divine concurrence in the production of creaturely effects—is implicated even at this level.

35. Duncan, *Proof*, chapters 5 and 8.

and states of creatures that belong to them by nature[36]) or of causae in fieri that realize, or actualize, the potentialities of other creatures that they possess in virtue of their capacities through the exercise of causal influence. In every case, then, the action of God as per se sustaining cause accounts for the continuous existence of the creature (its persistence in being), whereas the creature's properties are accounted for by reference to its essence and the way in which it is affected by the other things with which it interacts. As such, divine conservation acts not as an efficient cause on what we might call the "horizontal plane of causal influence" and interaction in which we account for the *becoming* of creatures but, instead, as causa in esse of the being of the creature. In so doing, it exercises a kind of *vertical* causal influence of a different order altogether, one compatible with the notion that whatever is involved in the details of the becoming of the creature can be accounted for in terms of efficient causes operating on the horizontal level of causal analysis. *How* a thing comes to be what it is ("becomes" in that sense) is determined by nature and environmental influence; *that* a thing comes to be what it becomes *at all* is due to its continuous creation by the First Cause.[37]

Considered with regard to its persistence in being, a thing's causa in esse is its per se sustaining cause, the activity of which is simultaneous to and continuous with respect to its effect and which, being withdrawn, is sufficient to extinguish the being of the effect. In other words, if God's divine conservation of a created thing is removed, then that thing will be automatically annihilated, reverting to nonexistence. Thus, on the traditional view of divine conservation, for God to annihilate a thing (reduce it to nothing) does not require any new positive action on God's part. On the contrary, it is merely the automatic consequence of God's decision to cease to conserve that thing in being. This is enacted simply by the withdrawal of God's creative causality from that thing, a necessary condition for its substantial unity and therefore of its continued existence. Thus, God's annihilation of an existing thing is the result of a *negative* action on God's part amounting to his *ceasing* to do something he was

36. This will include both their *capacities* (by means of which they are liable to be changed) and their *powers* (by means of which they are able to effect changes either in themselves or in other things).

37. The foregoing may well help to make sense of Aquinas's claim that God, the First Cause, and secondary causes are each the complete cause of the creature, though each in a different order, and Farrer's difficult notion of "double agency;" Farrer, *Faith and Speculation*, especially chapters 4 and 6.

doing previously. God withdraws his sustaining power from a creature and thus annihilates it simply by willing to cease sustaining it. Like creation and conservation, annihilation is the direct, transeunt effect of an immanent act of the divine will; the difference consists in the fact that, while creation and conservation are positive actions, annihilation is a negative action consisting in a negative state of affairs functioning as a negative cause, i.e., the privation of a necessary condition for some creature's persistence in being.

Focusing on conservation for a moment, it must be noted that while *at some point* divine conservation must be directly and immediately applied to created substances, it can also be (and typically is) *mediated* by the simultaneous presence and operation of other created beings or substances. In the case of created substances such as ourselves, for example, we find that there are many necessary conditions for our existence at every moment that we exist, the removal of any of which would immediately destroy us as embodied beings. We require the presence of oxygen, a stable temperature, gravitational influence that is neither too strong nor too weak, food, water, and so on in order to sustain ourselves in being. As I have argued elsewhere, any such set of conditions must terminate in an *unconditioned conditioner*, a being in whom essence and existence are identical; however, this does not rule out that between the *termini* of such a series there might be intermediate steps.[38] What I want to suggest in this context is that such a series could involve the *mind* or *soul* as the last intermediate step of a series of per se causes terminating in states of the body. This is to say that the mind, possessed of its own power of agency, serves as the local, direct per se sustaining cause of bodily states and processes and uses this causal influence to enact its free choices.

According to this view, the soul is the principle of life in the body, not as some sort of quasi-physical force operating in it as an efficient cause (such as *animal spirits*, *chi*, or *élan vital* were conceived to be by classical vitalists). Instead, the soul functions as the last intermediate, or *proximate per se* cause, directly sustaining the body's ongoing operations and processes, without which influence bodily life would cease. Just as God is causa in esse of the existence and persistence of things (whether immediately or mediately as the first and highest cause in the hierar-

---

38. Grisez, *Beyond the New Theism*, chapter 5, 59–84. This is essentially the point made by Grisez. I have developed this argument more fully in another manuscript.

chy of per se causes), effecting the whole being of every created thing without affecting it in the manner of an efficient cause, so too is the soul the principle of life in the body by sustaining its ongoing life processes after the manner of a per se cause. Just as the exercise of divine creative causality is consistent with the possibility that whatever happens at the horizontal level can be explained in terms of a combination of a thing's essence, or nature, and the results of its interaction with other things, so too is the operation of the soul as principle of life consistent with the notion that every state and process going on in the body can be accounted for in terms of nature and nurture, i.e., the combination of that living thing's genetic inheritance and the influence of its environment. That an organism's life takes the shape that it does is a consequence of nature and nurture; that it is alive *at all* is due to (at least proximately) to its soul. In this sense and in this sense alone, we may say that the soul is the "substantial form of the body"—not of the body *qua* material thing but instead precisely as *organism,* or *living* thing, as opposed to a corpse, which after all is a body, too, in its own way, possesses DNA, and so on. As such, we will not find the soul by searching the body for a quasi-physical "extra" something that directly produces bodily states without physical antecedents; its causal influence is of the vertical rather than horizontal variety and thus is not detectable on the horizontal level.[39]

I have argued elsewhere that to be a self, ego, or I is, as Descartes would put it, to be a *res cogitans,* i.e., a self-conscious, rational subject, and that to be such a subject is the intermittent characteristic of a certain sort of soul, the rational soul. The human *organism*, however, is the *combination* of body and soul, something greater than the sum of its parts. A body is alive, hence an organism, only by the presence of a soul; a soul is capable (in ordinary circumstances) of consciousness, hence of personhood only because it is related to a unique instance of a body possessing a particular kind of brain.[40] Inasmuch as soul and body are fully conceiv-

---

39. This also explains how an enduring subject without temporal parts can have a causal effect in a spatio-temporal material world—more on this below.

40. There is a sense, then, in which the existence of consciousness is dependent on the body and, in particular, the brain, since the intentional field of consciousness is the joint product of both soul and body. However, I follow the mainstream tradition in holding that the body, including the brain, is what Aristotle would have called a "moved mover" and Descartes a "machine," possessing only Reidian passive powers. Only the soul is a self-mover, possessing active powers of constitution and agency. The body (including the brain) is very much the junior partner in this enterprise. To study con-

able apart from one another, they are, according to Descartes, separate and independently existing substances with mutually exclusive natures. However, even though they are separate in existence, they are *by their very natures mutually dependent in operation*; neither is (nonmiraculously) capable of exercising its characteristic operations in the absence of the other. In relation to each other, then, each is a substance in its own right; in relation to the organism they jointly constitute, however, each is merely an incomplete, dependent part of the whole. Neither owes its existence to the other, nor can either produce the other. Nevertheless, at the same time, each is as though made for the other and thus incapable of functioning apart from the unity they jointly constitute, the organism, a *composite substance* with two other substances—mind and body—as its proper parts. It is thus the proper subject to which operations of both parts are properly ascribed: I think, I feel, I see, I bleed, I laugh, I walk, I sleep, I die, and so on.[41]

Of course, the soul as the per se cause of the vital processes of the body operates in a manner that is largely independent of willful control and of which we are not conscious (at least in normal circumstances). Indeed, we would have little reason to suppose that there was any such intermediate per se cause of bodily life if the soul were nothing more than what Aristotle conceived it to be. It is primarily due to conscious mind and the role of agency in causing our characteristic actions that we even have such a concept. To explain how, on the foregoing picture, free choice can come to be enacted in bodily states and behaviors is another matter, one that (as I have argued) forms part of our everyday experience of ourselves. Let us now turn to that part of the story.

---

sciousness and its contents by studying the brain is like attempting to appreciate music by studying the mechanical operation of one's stereo equipment. Further, any brain activity that is not to be accounted for in terms of mechanical causes may simply be the brain's reflection of mental activity occurring in consciousness. If that is so, there is no reason in principle that neuroscientists might not be able to "read" people's thoughts by monitoring their brains, even if substance dualism is true.

41. Strawson, *Individuals*, 81–113, especially 101-9. I believe that this account of Descartes' position on mind/body relation is similar to and compatible with that outlined in Skirry, *Descartes and Metaphysics*. However, the notion of vertical, as opposed to horizontal, causation is absent from his account.

3

The Exercise of Agency

HOW FREE WILL WORKS

The foregoing has established that there is an experiential presumption in favor of free will understood as the power to choose between open alternatives and that determinism, no matter how construed, is so problematic as to be of doubtful coherence. None of this is of much value, however, unless we can make sense of the notion of agency by providing an account of how free choice actually operates, one that coheres both with our experience of agency and with the modern scientific picture of the world. In my case, this means that the solution must be articulated within a traditional Cartesian dualist framework. According to this conception, the soul is an immaterial substance not subject to the laws of nature and the body a material thing, every physical state of which is fully explicable *as such* solely as the product of prior states of the universe governed by those laws. The seemingly insurmountable difficulty here lies in our inability, at least at first glance, to make sense of any sort of interaction between these two disparate substances. Yet I will argue that this can be done.

Given the foregoing, the following would seem to be *desiderata* for any plausible account of the exercise of agency:

1. The exercise of agency must be an intentional, conscious act of an agent who is an empirical (as opposed to a noumenal) self.

2. This act must be directly and immediately under the conscious control of the agent.

3. This act must be an immanent act of consciousness without any physical correlate.

4. Nevertheless, this immanent act must have an indirect transeunt effect on the body/brain by means of which it gives rise to some further state of the body.[1]

The first *desideratum* excludes any account of free will that supposes that the exercise of agency is affected by some mechanism or subject whose operations are inaccessible to ordinary consciousness, such as Kant's "noumenal self," or any account according to which the brain plays this role. This is an idea that some recent defenders of free will have tried to develop, but it is little comfort to think that some free agent causes my actions if that agent is not my (empirical) self, i.e., the self that I actually experience in everyday conscious experience. The second desideratum makes the power of agency and the act by means of which that power is exercised something that I can do immediately just through willing it and whose primary effect does not require any intervening mechanism to produce. This, in turn, requires the third desideratum, according to which the exercise of agency is wholly an immanent mental act, one occurring solely within consciousness and existing *as such* only there. The fourth desideratum, however, is required in order for the exercise of agency to have an influence either upon the states of my brain or on my externally observable behavior. Obviously, since according to the third desideratum, the exercise of agency is exclusively mental, it cannot affect anything directly in the physical world; however, I shall argue that the fourth desideratum can be met if we reconceive the way in which causal interaction between mind and brain produces bodily effects by an indirect influence.

Let me explain. Since the time of Descartes and largely due to his influence, it has been customary to think of efficient causation on an impact model of influence. Motion, for example, is thought to be something that is transferred from one body to another as the consequence of direct impact in which a "quantity of motion" preexisting in the causing body is transferred to the affected body, thereby giving rise to an observable effect. For example, a body at rest begins to move, or a body already

---

1. Double, *Non-Reality of Free Will*, 218–21. Double offers a list of six such desiderata for a theory of free will: the conceptual clarity condition, the empirical plausibility condition, the extension condition, the ability-to-choose-otherwise condition, the control condition, and the rationality condition. He further maintains that no extant theory of free will can meet these conditions. I believe the theory to be sketched here does succeed in meeting them on any reasonable construal of those conditions; however, I will not discuss this here.

in motion is deflected from the path it would otherwise follow because of its contact with the first. Further, all observable objects are thought to be composed from simple material particles characterized by a few basic physical properties in such a manner that all of the gross observable features of those bodies can be accounted for in terms of the interaction of those irreducible parts. All change is ultimately reducible to change of place: *motus* (change-in-general) becomes *motion*, (i.e., what the Aristotelians called "local motion," or change of place) the subject of the branch of physics known as "mechanics." In the world as described by the New Physics, there is consequently no room for any immaterial influences, such as substantial forms or final causes, in the production of observable events. Whatever is not physical/material, such as the ideas of externally existing material bodies produced in sense perception, exists only in the immaterial soul or mind. To this extent, Descartes adheres to the New Physics.

At the same time, as we saw in chapter 2, it is quite clear from our everyday experience of ourselves as conscious subjects that ends, purposes, and goals (i.e., final causes) play a very large part both in our experience of ourselves as agents and in our understanding of the behavior of others understood as the products of their own agency. Far from being a sort of theory or the consequence of some sort of theoretical apparatus, it is instead a set of *facts*, or *data*, that no plausible theory of mind can plausibly ignore. However, if we are not simply to ignore that data, we must find some way to account for it within the categories of the New Science. Failing that, we must modify that picture in order to accommodate those facts which, after all, we apprehend with greater clarity and certainty than the truth of any scientific theory, no matter how well confirmed it may seem to be. Of course, the simplistic mechanical picture of nature provided by Cartesian and Newtonian physics has long since been superseded in natural science; however, most people, even most philosophers, continue to be wedded to some version of the Galilean physicalist picture of the external world.[2]

Applied to the exercise of agency, we have the classic problem of mind/body interaction insofar as mind is supposed to influence body. In Descartes' case, Princess Elisabeth of Bohemia put the point most strongly in her initial letter to that philosopher. While she could imagine

---

2. I have criticized this thesis in detail in other, unpublished manuscripts; for a précis of this critique, see Duncan, "Is Neuroscience Possible?" posted to *PhilPapers*.

one body causally influencing another in the way the New Science of her day explained it (in terms of contact and transfer of motion as described above), she could not see how this, the only model for efficient causation available within that science, could be applied to mind/body interaction.[3] Descartes himself had insisted that soul (i.e., conscious mind) and body were different substances precisely because they were diverse in nature.[4] In so doing, Elisabeth suggested, Descartes had cut off any possibility for conceiving how either could exert any influence on the other. For later critics of dualism, the problem was even clearer: either the physical world is a closed causal system or it is not. If it is, then the conservation laws rule out the possibility that the soul could either introduce energy into the system or even so much as move that energy around somehow. If it is not, then we ought to be able to detect this nonphysical energy when it is introduced into the brain from outside—and we do not.

Descartes gives his response to these objections in his reply to Elisabeth's second letter; I still regard it as perfectly adequate, despite the fact that it gives us much less than we would like to have.[5] Essentially, Descartes invokes a principle I have elsewhere called the "experiential presumption" (or EP for short): the prima facie best explanation for anything *appearing* to be X is that it *is* X. According to Descartes, the facts are clear. We *are* minds, we *have* bodies, and each of these is a separately existing substance. At the same time, they are much more closely associated with one another than, say, a pilot and a ship might be. Our everyday experience informs us clearly that acts of choice are the cause of many of our externally observable bodily behaviors and that the experiential contents of our mental states of sense perception are the causal products of the influence of external bodies on our own.[6] While there are both mental processes and bodily processes involved in the production of our bodily behavior, the influence of mind on body (and, for that matter, body on mind) is quite clearly direct, immediate, and unique. As such, there is no prospect of further explaining this relation by specifying a mechanism capable of bridging the gap between the two. At best, any other causal process occurring in nature is going to provide an analogy too distant to be useful in attempting to understand what is

3. Shapiro, *Correspondence*, 62.
4. CSM, vol. 2, 54.
5. Shapiro, *Correspondence*, 63–67.
6. Ibid., 64; see also 69–70.

happening in the case of mind/body relation. Descartes speculated that perhaps he could lessen the mystery by isolating the point of contact to one spot in the brain (the pineal gland) and limiting it to one kind of influence (the "stimulation" of the "animal spirits"), and he was clearly wrong about this. However, his main point still stands.

As I interpret Descartes (i.e., by reference to what he actually said to Elisabeth, rather than what we moderns think he should or could have said), he was claiming that there is an experiential presumption in favor of dualist interactionism inasmuch as the evident facts find their most natural explanation in accordance with its principles.[7] By contrast, its major opponents, idealism and physicalism, both require that our experience of ourselves and of our world is systematically misleading. Idealism (which requires that we discount our apparent experience of the body and the external world and reinterpret that experience in terms of mental processes and their contents) is clearly more plausible than its more popular materialist rival because it recognizes the phenomenological facts of conscious experience. For the materialist or physicalist philosopher of mind, it is consciousness-as-experienced that is somehow illusory or the product of some sort of delusion and in need of reduction or elimination; as I argued earlier, there is little reason to suppose that this sort of program will succeed. *Every* account of mind/body interaction breaks down at the *same point*, viz., at precisely the point where the theory has to specify the *exact* relation between mind and body, i.e., between myself qua self-conscious subject and myself qua embodied being. There is nothing unique to Cartesian dualism in this. Thus, the experiential presumption in favor of dualism remains undefeated and thus continues to deserve our credence.

As I say, I am for the most part satisfied with this response. In this chapter, however, I intend to do more—even though, given the foregoing, it is not necessary to do so—by specifying the nature of mind/body interaction in the case of intentional action. In this case, then, we are concerned with how the exercise of agency produces intentional action involving some bodily state or affect that realizes that action in the external, physical world. The key to this account is to reconceive the causal relation between mind and body and its mode of influencing the body. What follows is the beginning of that account.

---

7. Garber, *Descartes Embodied*, 168–88.

A MODEL FOR FREE CHOICE

So far, I have suggested that the causal influence of the soul on the body consists in its general role of sustaining bodily states and operations as an intermediate per se cause or causa in esse of the body qua living thing, or organism. Although intermediate in the order of such causes that terminate in God as First Cause and Unconditioned Conditioner, it is nevertheless the last in the series of vertical, or per se, causes whose influence is applied directly to the conservation of bodily states. It is the proximate per se cause of the life of the body. It is in the relation between soul and body that we will most likely find the proper account of how freedom of choice is possible, and this is where I will claim to have found it. As such, the first point that I wish to make in this context is a phenomenological one: *intentional action is such primarily by the fact that it proceeds to enactment in bodily behavior through the medium of consciousness.* That is to say, intentional action—action willfully undertaken by someone—implies the medium of consciousness by its very nature. A bit of behavior hardly counts as an intentional action unless the person who engages in it is (at a bare minimum) aware *that* he is doing it and has some conception of *why* he is doing it.[8] In the paradigm case, as we have seen, the action will be intentional in the full-blown sense that involves deliberation and choice, mental acts that precede their enactment in bodily behavior. Further, a good deal of the externally observable behavior we exhibit, and certainly that part to which we attach the greatest significance, constitutes intentional action in that sense. In particular, it is with regard to action of this sort that we are most inclined to claim that we are free. Of course, much of our behavior is routine, habitual, and hardly even attended to by the agents who perform it. Nevertheless, this sort of behavior is often in aid of, or partially constitutive of, intentional action. For example, How many steps did I take when I entered this room in order to sit at my desk? I don't know. I wasn't counting my steps as I entered the room. Even so, my entering the room and walking across it to my desk were part of an intentional action

---

8. It does not follow from this that I can be held responsible only for my intentional actions or that I can be held responsible for any action that I intentionally perform. The relation between intentionality and responsibility is a difficult one and a topic that cannot be broached here. Further, the vexed question of whether externally observable behaviors that do not constitute intentional actions are nonactions or a different kind, or class, of action will not be taken up here. Nothing in what follows hangs on how we decide these issues.

that I deliberately and willfully performed for a particular end of which I was explicitly aware, i.e., precisely so I could write the words that you are reading now.

Intentional actions of the sort that we are likely to want to describe as paradigmatically free, hence for which we can be held unambiguously and directly responsible, are those that proceed to enactment through the medium of consciousness. In the same way, we are likely to regard those actions which we do involuntarily (as when acting under the aegis of an irresistible impulse) or unconsciously (as when sleepwalking or hypnotized) or which we do "without thinking" (i.e., without adverting to them) are non-intentional. As such, we are only indirectly responsible for them—and that typically only if we can trace those actions to an earlier action that was intentional in the full-blown sense.[9] If determinism is true, however, it hardly seems to make any difference whether or not my actions are intentional in the above sense, since according to that theory, my conscious awareness of what I am doing is, from the point of view of the *causes* of my action, merely *epiphenomenal*. As I have argued at length, if determinism is true, conscious awareness plays no ineliminable, indeed, no substantive role at all in the explanation of what I do.[10] At best, one might think that the question of whether or not an action of mine is intentional determines whether my behavior will be most readily changed by punishing me or someone else or no one. Once again, however, determinism seems out of step with what we experience when we take the first-person point of view of the agent seriously. From that point of view, we must regard our conscious awareness as not merely the medium of intentional action, but rather as at least partly explanatory of what we do and thus as a genuine *causal* factor in its production.

At the same time, we hardly create our actions ex nihilo from within consciousness itself. Instead, experience teaches us that the introduction of potential objects of choice and action into consciousness is a spontaneous affair and thus that the origins of our actions with regard to their initial presence in consciousness are to be found in processes and states of affairs lying outside our immediate conscious control. The primary

---

9. For example, a drunkard or a drug addict may currently be so in the grips of his addiction that there is nothing that he will not do in order to acquire the means to satisfy his by now irresistible habit. However, since his addiction is the result of earlier free choices, he can still be held responsible for the crimes he now (we are supposing) cannot help but commit.

10. Duncan, "Thinking" and "Strange Case," both posted to *PhilPapers*.

motives prompting us to act—appetite, desire, passions, and the projects they suggest to us—arise in us spontaneously and, through making an unbidden and powerful claim upon our attention, propose various potential actions to us. Some, like appetite, are directly grounded in our physiology and expressive of our instinctual drives, needing no external prompting in order to appear in consciousness, despite generally having them. Others, like desire and passion, are intentional in that they are focused on an object and are typically expressive of a judgment that may (but need not) involve an acquired disposition, or *habit*. Beyond these, there is also a large variety of acquired tastes, aversions, and states of character (such as virtues and vices), disposing us to act in numerous ways. Beyond even these, there are large-scale *moods* or *outlooks*, such as cheerfulness, pessimism, irritability, and so on that color one's entire view of life and which are generally regarded as "constitutional," i.e., something not chosen by us but to some extent modifiable by "moral effort." It is not up to me to decide to become a constitutionally cheerful, as opposed to a morose or gloomy, person simply by making a one-time act of will or simply to will to acquire a taste for yams when the mere smell of them cooking produces a gag reflex in me. Nor (Dickens notwithstanding) does it seem possible to become an honest and generous man after a lifetime of mendacity and penny-pinching in the space of a single night or to (nonmiraculously) cease to feel the prick of sexual appetite simply by resolving to swear off sex forever, as disappointed lovers sometimes do. If these changes were even possible for us, it would be very hard work indeed for us to accomplish them.

The foregoing factors dictate, in large part, how (and how well) I will react to what goes on around me and therefore what actions will appear attractive to me under the circumstances. In many cases, there will be a choice that strikes us as *obvious* even without the consideration of alternatives and which we will then proceed to do without deliberation—though the obvious action will not be the same for every person. An ancient Greek soldier who sees the enemy breaching the wall near his position may rush to the defense of his city if he were one sort of person, drop his sword and surrender if he were another, or scream and run away if he were yet a third. In situations of choice where we have the leisure to deliberate, there may be more than one alternative that attracts us enough to merit our consideration, even though they will rarely attract us with equal force. Liberty of indifference does not (despite the name) indicate that the felt, or "psychic," pull of each alternative is equally balanced. In most cases, there will be an alternative that we feel most strongly, and it is a safe generalization of folk psychology that we most often do what we most want to do in the circumstances. The roots of action, then, are bodily and realized in our motivational structures insofar as these are sensibly seen as located in our central nervous system and the muscles it controls, all of which are rooted in the brain; the promptings of that structure are not directly under our conscious control and are not chosen by us.

One way of conceptualizing individual actions as realized in bodily states and processes is Farrer's notion of the "action-pattern." An action-pattern is the root of an overt action as expressed in observable behavior as that action exists dispositionally in the central nervous system. In appropriate circumstances, the action-pattern is triggered, or brought to life and, subsequent to that triggering, becomes an object of conscious awareness.[11] In most cases of irresistible impulse, conscious awareness simply registers the presence in consciousness of that impulse and experiences being "carried away" by its force in a manner it is helpless to resist, to arrest, or to redirect.

In others, consciousness is bypassed altogether, and the victim experiences a "blackout." However, occurrences of this sort are surely quite rare, and most of the cases we describe in this way involve a metaphorical, or hyperbolic, use of language rather than a literal assertion. Indeed, I myself have never experienced this sort of psychological compulsion, although I do not doubt that it exists. The great majority of the action-patterns that we are consciously aware of as "coming to life" in us appear to us to be resistible even if we do not make any effort to do so. Further, the great majority of action-patterns that prompt us to their enactment we routinely resist in such a way that they never are enacted in overt behavior.

---

11. Although the "action potential" precedes the action only by milliseconds, scientists are able to trace the action-pattern further back than this, so that it is possible to predict with fair accuracy, even apparently free choices, up to ten seconds prior to our consciously making them, at least in simple cases. I am inclined to think that this merely confirms the fact that the "coming to life" of the action-pattern in the brain precedes our awareness of that action-pattern in consciousness as a desirable alternative, perhaps among others. The deterministic implications drawn by some researchers and suggested in popular accounts of these experiments are surely too quick. For more discussion of this, see Mele, *Effective Intentions*, 49–90.

Nevertheless, we may suppose that from the perspective of external, third-person observation there will be no observable difference between an action-pattern that embodies an irresistible impulse and one that embodies an impulse that we experience as resistible. In each case, there will be an unbroken series of bodily events and processes leading from external bodily stimulation to the formation of a brain state embodying the recognition of the significance of that stimulation for the conscious agent so stimulated. This will result in the arising of a response in the form of a "reactive" brain state capable of giving rise to an external behavior relevant to the stimulus to which it constitutes a reaction and which is subsequently enacted in external behavior. A waitress in a café places a cup of coffee in plain view before me, and desiring to drink coffee, I reach out to take the cup, raise it to my lips, and drink. A complete, seamless, psychophysical story of this event, beginning with light waves leaving the coffee cup and ending with the coffee entering my mouth can be told from the perspective of external observation. According to this story, each distinguishable step in the process can be understood as the product of prior physical causes, efficient causes constituting the physically sufficient conditions for the behavior we observe and refer to as "drinking coffee." There are no gaps here that need to be filled by something called "free will," despite the fact that I would regard this act of drinking coffee to be voluntary, rather than compelled, and the impulse to do so eminently resistible. If there is free will or human agency, therefore, we will not find it at the level of the action-pattern as physically realized in the body. Nor should we look for it on the level of ordinary, third-person observation of the sort that psychologists depend on.

Nevertheless, none of these familiar facts (or, at any rate, plausible speculations) rules out the possibility of free choice. In every case where we have the opportunity to pause and deliberate, it is always possible for me to consider whether to do as I am prompted to do by the impulse of the moment or to do otherwise. Even where only one potential action is in view, it is always possible in principle for me to choose *not* to do it, so long as the impulse *inclines without necessitating*, i.e., is resistible for me in the circumstances.[12] As such, the fact that I do not resist many of the

---

12. Or to not choose to do it, which is something distinct from choosing not to do it and may be a distinction that makes a difference in some cases, especially with regard to what we might call "nonactions" or "*omissions*" that produce preventable effects. See the next footnote.

impulses that prompt me to act does not make them any the less free, just so long as I could have chosen to resist them.[13] What still needs to be provided, however, is an account of how this resistance is accomplished, and in so doing, positive free choices are enacted. I will now attempt to explain how this works.

I previously stated that the relation between the soul functioning as the substantial form of the body and the bodily operations it sustains is that of the immediately operating per se sustaining cause of the body qua living thing, or organism. Most of the bodily states and processes that fall under its purview are not consciously accessible to introspection. However, experience teaches us that some of these states, for example, those constituting action-patterns (at least in normal circumstances) enter nontrivially into consciousness as spontaneously arising impulses to act in various ways in the current circumstances as those circumstances

---

By *incline without necessitating*, I mean to indicate a phenomenological feature of most projects that recommend themselves to us as potential objects of choice, i.e., that they command only part of my attention, not the whole of it. Even if a project has greater motivational force, or "psychic pull," than its rivals, to the extent that this leaves conscious space for the consideration of alternatives, it is possible for us to mediatize its influence by concentration of attention, focusing either on one of the alternatives or by considering the alternative itself "in a different light," i.e., considering it from a less attractive point of view. By contrast, irresistible impulses either bypass consciousness altogether or, even if present in and to consciousness, so occupy it that it leaves no memory afterwards, or is precisely felt as irresistible, as in the case of a heroin addict's craving for that drug.

13. This will not always be sufficient to prevent the behavior itself from arising. Many philosophers have discussed Frankfurt-style cases in which my choice *not* to do X will inevitably give rise to my doing X due to the operation of some compulsive mechanism. However, even in those cases in which I am aware that such a mechanism exists, I still have it within my power to decide whether the behavior is elicited by that mechanism or through my own agency. If I freely choose to do it through my own agency, then I am clearly responsible for my action, despite the fact that I would have been compelled to do it against my will even if I choose not to do it. On the other alternative, whether I am culpable in such cases will depend upon my motives. For example, if I deliberately form an intention not to do X in order to "trip" the mechanism and thereby evade responsibility for my act, it is arguable that since I did this knowingly and willingly, I am still responsible for the action, but not otherwise, since causal forces outside of my control produced it. Further, if I attempt to evade the mechanism by putting off a decision, i.e., simply by not choosing either to do or refrain from doing X, but fail in this attempt (since the mechanism was designed to account for this possibility), then, in that case, I did not choose to do the action, and the mechanism operates like an irresistible impulse. Then, in that case, I would not be responsible for the action precisely because forces outside of my control unavoidably caused it.

are apprehended by the agent experiencing those impulses. These states will typically involve perception and judgment focused on an object and giving rise to a desire or passion motivating us to respond to that situation in some way. Of course, the situation envisaged may be remote, as in a young person deciding about a future career, or merely hypothetical, as when one amuses oneself by imagining what one would do if one were somehow to become the President of the United States. However, in this context we will focus on those situations in which genuine choice is both possible to effect and accompanied by some urgency.

Intentional actions, as I have said, are realized through the medium of consciousness, and it is here that we should look for any possible causal influence of mind on the body. Since, as I have also concluded, this influence is not to be found at the horizontal level of efficient causation, where purely mechanical explanation seems sufficient so far as we know, we must suppose instead that the mind's causal influence on the body is analogous to that exercised by God in sustaining and annihilating created substances. What I am suggesting here is that the mind's power of agency, exercised through the medium of consciousness, selects among the alternatives available to it by sustaining some of these and failing to sustain others, allowing some of these action-patterns to achieve full-blown realization in concrete, observable bodily behavior and preventing others from doing so. To conceive of this possibility is to suggest that an action-pattern is not merely present in consciousness but, in doing so, becomes *dependent upon consciousness* for its forward progress into full-blown action, the mind or soul acting as its per se sustaining cause.[14] To those action-patterns to which we deny that sustaining power, forward progress thereby is denied. The normal course of events in the material world will not give rise to the action that would have resulted if the mind had acted to sustain that project.[15] Let us now

---

14. After all, as I noted earlier in chapter 1, I can simply refrain from doing anything, in which case none of the alternatives that I consider need ever be realized in overt behavior; as such, there is no necessity in my performing *any* action whatsoever in those cases, hence no need for there to be a "winner" among competing projects.

15. As I noted above, I believe that this account of mental causation is consistent in principle with a "gapless" neuropsychology, according to which there are neither breaks in the causal sequence leading from initial "stimulation" to the eventual "behavioral output" nor the necessity of postulating any macroscopically significant quantum indeterminacy in the brain in order to make free action possible. In one sense, the beauty of this is that, from the perspective of those who limit themselves to the third-person point of view on action, everything will appear as if determinism is true. It is only from

consider this proposal within the context of a phenomenology of the exercise of agency.

In many cases when I deliberate, my intentional field of consciousness is distributed among competing alternatives. At a bare minimum, there are the alternatives either to do or to refrain from doing X. In that case, I have three basic choices available to me: to do X, not to do X, or to put off making a decision (i.e., not to choose either to do or refrain from doing X). In those cases in which there is some urgency imposed on my choice, the latter will often have the same effect as choosing not to do X. As I deliberate over my alternatives, I will consider each of them from various perspectives, perhaps trying them on for size. After having sorted out my impulses in reflective equilibrium and having determined which of the alternatives is most attractive on the whole, as well as considering whatever relevant reasons for and against each project that may have occurred to me, I make a *practical judgment* about which alternative is best for me to do under the circumstances. This judgment involves consent to a proposition and can be considered correct or incorrect when judged either from the perspective of the agent's own intentions or from the perspective of an ideal observer possessing all the knowledge relevant to the situation of choice. Whether one is culpable or not for an erroneous judgment will depend on a number of factors; however, we cannot go into this topic here.

All of this is possible because, being an immaterial substance, or soul, I am also a rational being, one capable of apprehending propositional contents and their logical relations to other contents and thus able to make judgments on that basis as to the likely truth of those claims. Since, as a rational being, I naturally seek truth, the fact that I apprehend a proposition as rationally justified on the basis of other propositions that I also believe to be true, therefore, inclines me to believe it. Further, among those propositions that I entertain are candidates for belief about what, given my situation and circumstances, ought to be done and their applicability to my own case. Since, as a rational being, I am naturally

---

the first-person point of view (which, as we saw in the last two chapters, is more directly and more certainly apprehended by me than any scientific theory) that we are able to grasp the fact that our actions are the results of our free choices. As such, it is the third-person point of view on action that bids fair to be illusory rather than our experience of agency. Thus, the foregoing preserves the illusion of determinism without admitting that the third-person point of view is the only one relevant to the understanding of human action. Determinists should be well able to appreciate the irony of this result.

out for the good and see these practical judgments as leading me to that end, I will naturally be inclined to act in accordance with them. Nothing prevents me from acting in accordance with judgments of this sort. However, since abstract objects, such as propositions, arguments, and judgments, are not causes, neither do they ineluctably cause my action. Instead, I retain the power either to act on this inclination or to act from some contrary, nonrational motive, such as self-love, perceived self-interest, appetite, passion, or desire also in play at that time. If I do the former, then my action, being rationally justified, is blameless and, to the extent that I act, not just in conformity with reason, but rather from reason, is worthy of praise and reward. If I do the latter, then my action, undertaken with deliberate and willful disregard for the good I know I ought to do/pursue, is blameworthy, an appropriate object of censure, and if a severe enough dereliction, of punishment as well. In both cases, the reason is the same: I chose to do what I did in circumstances in which I could have resisted (or at least tried to resist) the inclination on which I acted.

Nevertheless, experience teaches us that our practical judgments, whether correct or incorrect, deliberate or casual, do not always govern our actions; we often act against what we consciously acknowledge to be our best judgment. Thus, even though our practical judgments are (ideally at least) *not* free, being an ideally rational response to the situation of choice that determinately selects a single alternative, nevertheless my actions *are* free because I can decline to enact the alternative to which that judgment bids me. As such, there is more to the phenomenology of free choice than mere deliberation and practical judgment. There is also the act of *choice* itself, i.e., the mental act of making a *decision*, or selecting among competing projects. This act of choice is another distinct mental act, independent of practical judgment and not always guided by it. It is also a *free act*, one which, though rooted in a concrete situation and informed by both nonrational motivation and the guidance of reason, is nevertheless incapable of being reduced to any of those factors, either individually or jointly, as a sufficient explanation in the order of efficient causality. Indeed, it is the paradigmatically free act; all other acts we describe as free are such due to their being the consequence of free choice.

With regard to the act of free choice, we cannot ask the question "Why did you do it?" in the sense of "What caused you to do it?"—only in the sense of "What made you think you were justified in doing it?" The *explanation* for an act of choice is given, not in terms of productive causes, but rather in terms of justifying reasons that make it clear that the choice was the best one under the circumstances or, if this is obviously not the case, why it appeared to the agent to be so. Failing this, we may conclude that the agent acted irrationally, due to the influence of an improperly organized motivational structure, and specify those influences by reference to the agent's moods, desires, passions, habits, and overall character, all of which were (we are supposing) resistible in the circumstances but which the agent chose not to resist. Only if we see the resulting behavior as the result of an irresistible impulse (and, further, an irresistible impulse that cannot be traced in any significant way to prior free choices, such as a sudden onset of insanity due to a chemical imbalance in the brain) do we conclude that the behavior is not an intentional action at all, but simply the result of the operation of purely physical causes. In this case, of course, the behavior can be explained by reference to efficient causes beyond the power of the agent to anticipate or control; however, just by that very fact, it does not count as an intentional action. One is thus neither to be praised nor blamed for having done it, though one may be an appropriate object of pity in such circumstances.

Free choice is a wholly mental and—when made with fully conscious consent of the will—*cognitive* act, one for which we can in principle be held responsible, although there may be cases in which responsibility can be mitigated or even altogether removed. By contrast, nonrational animals, though sometimes punished in order to influence their subsequent behavior, can never be morally responsible for their behavior because they are not capable of free choice. However, just because the act of free choice is a cognitive act, it is not capable by itself of enacting the behavior that realizes the act one has chosen to do. Not all of my free choices become enacted; sometimes I change my mind, sometimes I forget, sometimes I get distracted, and so on; on other occasions, my resolve fades away or is overcome by other nonrational elements of my motivational structure. For example, the teenager who has resolved to start a conversation with that cute girl he has a crush on suddenly finds himself turning shy and tongue-tied in her presence and so does not carry through on his resolve. The enactment of my free choice requires a further free act, traditionally known as "volition." It is volition that converts my free choice into external behavior. Volition is the natural complement of free choice understood as decision making: if I *choose* to do something, in ordinary circumstances, I *will to do* that thing. Hence, I can be said to *will* that act. Indeed, unless I fully intend to do that thing at the time I resolve to do it, there is a sense in which I did not really choose to do that thing after all. As such, in some cases we learn that it is useless for us to resolve to do something (i.e., to form an intention to do it, an intention that in normal circumstances constitutes a choice) precisely because experience has taught us that we simply lack the power to carry through on that resolve. However, this is hardly the standard case: I can choose to do something and have the power to enact that choice but simply fail to do so.[16]

Volition is clearly the key to the account of free will that I am presenting here. Yet how is volition possible? Farrer provides the key to this with his notion of *concentration of attention*. As I have argued elsewhere, one of the basic features of our cognitive power of introspection consists in our ability to direct our attention from one element of the intentional field of consciousness to another and from one aspect of any particular element of that field to another. It is just this feature that makes it possible for us to alter foreground and background in consciousness and to bring to full, explicit, conscious awareness ubiquitous features of consciousness that are normally background features of our intentional field of awareness and thus of which we are for the most part only implicitly and inchoately aware.[17] Concentration of attention, however, is not to be conceived of as a mysterious power to focus the light of consciousness on one object in preference to another. It is simply our common, everyday ability to attend to one element of consciousness in preference to another at our own discretion; it consists in a basic action brought about simply by willing it. It is also a free act in normal circumstances, although experience teaches us that this power is limited. While it is normally very easy for us to concentrate our attention simply by willing to do so, we have all experienced cases in which even our best effort to "put something out of our minds" is ineffectual—we just can't stop thinking about something or other, or we find ourselves easily distracted, tired and thus unable to concentrate, etc. However, we will

---

16. See Pieper, *Reality and the Good*, 55–90, 120, for a full account of all the stages in free action, from initial stimulation to enactment in externally observable behavior.

17. Duncan, *Proof*, 68–89.

here consider the standard case in which concentration of attention is easily accomplished.

My primary claim, and the key to my account of volition, is that concentration of attention is a matter of *disattending* to what we do not want to think about, rather than of focusing on that about which we wish to think. Concentration of attention is achieved by withdrawing our attention from what we no longer wish to hold in our minds, something that we ordinarily accomplish simply by *fiat*. *I just stop thinking about it, an action I accomplish directly and immediately, without doing anything else.* In this sense, concentration of attention is, for the human mind or soul, the complement of God's power of annihilation, a *negative* act consisting in my *ceasing* to do that which I was previously doing, rather than the initiation of a new act. In ordinary circumstances, that about which I cease to think "drops out" of centrality in consciousness, resulting in a change in the contents of the intentional field of conscious awareness and the relation of what is central and peripheral in conscious experience. When I deliberately stop thinking about something and succeed in so doing, something we commonly experience in everyday life, concentration of attention is the consequence of my acts of *disattention* to those elements of my mental life that I no longer wish to think about or entertain.

Volition, then, will be an act of disattention of this sort exercised with regard to contents of consciousness when those contents are action-patterns representing possible projects that it lies within my power to realize, or enact, in external behavior. An action-pattern can only blossom into an intentional action by proceeding to enactment in external behavior through the medium of consciousness. If I deny my attention to that action-pattern, its forward progress is blocked due to the lack of one of the necessary conditions for its further development. Volition enacts my choice by concentrating my attention on only one of the alternatives available to me at the time and does so by disattending to its competitors. The action-pattern that is sustained finds the path forward to ultimate enactment unblocked and so proceeds to full realization; the others, unable to proceed any further toward enactment, fail to be become my actions. Volition, itself a free act, thus expresses my free choice and constitutes the exercise of my power of agency. In this case, an immanent negative mental act of disattention gives rise to a transeunt, physical effect.

Volitions are not the only example of a negative state of affairs, i.e., ones without a positive realization in actuality, serving as causal factors in the production of positive, even physical, states of affairs. All that is required is that such states of affairs should constitute *significant lacks*, i.e., the lack of one or more of the necessary conditions for some physical process to occur. For example, lack of oxygen and lack of food, though negative states of affairs, produce death (cessation of biological life) in many organisms without acting as efficient causes of death (as electrocution or stabbing would be). In each case, there is undoubtedly an interesting tale to tell about how these significant lacks produce death through some immanent process occurring in an organism's body triggered by the lack in question. In principle, at least, we can expect some sort of story about what happens to action-patterns—however, these are constituted as states of the central nervous system—that fail to proceed through the medium of consciousness to enactment. This account will consist in the description of an immanent process occurring in the brain by means of which these rejected projects are dissipated, though it is not obvious that this story will be of any philosophical significance. If, as experience seems to testify, intentional action proceeds to enactment in behavior through the medium of consciousness, to deny one's conscious attention to any action-pattern effectively removes one of the necessary conditions for its enactment and is thus sufficient to prevent it from becoming one of my actions. It thus *explains* its failing to proceed to enactment in the same way that lack of food explains the death of someone who dies of starvation, something that might be listed as the cause of death on a death certificate. It thus can be called the "negative cause" of that action-pattern failing to be enacted, despite the fact that it is ontologically constituted only as a lack, rather than as or by a positive reality in its own right.

Thus, I have said that volition, by means of which I enact my free choice by disattending from its competitors while continuing to attend to the chosen project, resulting in concentration of attention on that chosen alternative, is a *negative* action. This is so because in disattending, I simply cease doing something that I was doing previously, i.e., entertaining that action-pattern as my potential action. This is something that experience teaches me that I can ordinarily accomplish simply by fiat. Despite being a negative action (a mere *ceasing to do*), it is nevertheless something that I do and which results in a real change in the contents of my intentional field of consciousness. By contrast, my "action" of sustaining the chosen project, while it involves the operation of the mind or soul as the immediate per se sustaining cause of one of the operations of a living body (in this case, an action-pattern as realized in states and processes occurring in the central nervous system), is not something I strictly speaking bring about except insofar as I refrain from interfering with an ongoing, preestablished process occurring in my brain. Unlike God, who has the power to produce real things ex nihilo by simple fiat, the introduction of action-patterns into consciousness is not something over which we have direct conscious control in most cases. We simply find that certain potential responses present themselves as likely effective/desirable responses to perceived situations and circumstances and thus recommend themselves to us for enactment. Since the mind or soul has already been sustaining the chosen project since its first introduction into consciousness, my volition, resulting in concentration of attention on the chosen alternative, adds nothing new to the mix. It simply consists in my *not ceasing to sustain* that alternative, i.e., not removing one of the necessary conditions for the enactment of that alternative. In relation to the *chosen* or *selected* project, then, volition is thus more accurately described as a *nonaction*, or *omission* (i.e., a failure to do an act that it lay within one's power to do), rather than a positive action, albeit a nonaction that constitutes a necessary condition for the realization of the action-pattern. In those cases where that condition, along with the other necessary conditions for enactment, are *jointly sufficient* for the enactment of that alternative in external bodily behavior, enactment results. In such case, the enacted alternative, at least with regard to its positive physical reality, finds a complete explanation in terms of the neurophysical conditions that give rise to it. Volition simply explains why this alternative rather than another was actualized in external behavior and does so in virtue of the fact that in the case of the enacted alternative and in its case alone, *all* the necessary conditions, mental as well as physical, were present. In no case, then, does the volition expressive of the power of agency in a particular instance act as an efficient cause on the horizontal level of event-production. It remains, in all its operations, firmly at the vertical level of per se/sustaining causation.[18]

Since volition is neither a physical nor a positive reality, it does not need an efficient cause. The negative act of disattention by means

---

18. To put this in Honderich's terms, my sustaining the project is part (the decisive part) of the causal circumstance that produces my action.

of which concentration of attention is accomplished is the immediate exercise of a basic power through my fiat with an immediate intramental effect, the very exercise of agency itself. Far from being mysterious or unintelligible, the exercise of agency so described is a familiar fact of everyday experience, neither capable of nor needing any further causal explanation. The capacity of the soul to act as the per se sustaining cause of states and processes occurring in the body of a living organism is part of the mind or soul's nature understood as the substantial form of the body and thus lies beyond the reach of physical explanation. At the same time, its existence is an evident fact of our experience since it can be interrupted in some cases by my act of will.

At the beginning of this chapter, I outlined a set of desiderata for any account of human agency, free will, or free choice. The account I have sketched here appears to me to meet all of these desiderata. The exercise of agency is shown to consist in volition, a negative act of disattention that removes one of the necessary conditions for the enactment of action-patterns that I have chosen not to enact and which results in the concentration of my attention on the alternative I have chosen. This negative act, having no positive reality and in no way acting as an efficient cause, operates without the need for any sort of physical realization at the horizontal level of efficient causation, hence is not plausibly identified with any state of the brain or any process occurring there. Nevertheless, volition is shown to be a perfectly familiar action that I can directly and immediately perform and which immediately gives rise to its immanent effect in consciousness. Further, this action has an indirect transeunt effect on the central nervous system inasmuch as it denies to all but one of the action-patterns physically realized there one of the necessary conditions required for them to proceed through consciousness to enactment in external bodily behavior. The foregoing is thus compatible with the idea that these acts possess irreducible causal powers capable of giving rise to genuine changes in the external world. In so doing, we have helped clarify the interaction relation between the soul and body as conceived within a Cartesian dualist account of the human person with regard to the production of human action, and in so doing, we have shown *how free will works*.[19]

---

19. On another occasion, I hope to provide the rest of the story, explaining the interaction relation involved in the production of mental contents because of bodily stimulation.

4

Sin and the Fall

THE MISUSE OF FREEDOM AND ITS AFTERMATH

SIN IS NOT A popular topic, and most of us would prefer not to think about it or, if so, simply to dismiss the idea indignantly. In our contemporary culture, we have so managed to submerge the sense of our own individual sinfulness that the very idea is foreign to most of us, including many "religious" people. The current generation, raised in a largely irreligious atmosphere, appears to have no inkling of it at all. Nevertheless, I contend that sin and sinfulness are still the essential fact of the human condition and its predicament, which we can never successfully address until we face, recognize, and accept these facts as facts. We are not OK. We are not autonomous. We are not in control. We are not automatically evolving toward a state of perfection in which we will leave poverty and injustice behind like a bad dream. Nothing—not Marx, Freud, or genetic engineering—is going to save us. Only God can save us and at that only if, through acceptance of his unmerited gift of grace, we repent and believe the Gospel.

Having said that, let me hasten to reassure the reader that I am not writing this chapter to preach, which I am not competent to do, but rather to philosophize, which is my stock in trade. For the most part, I will attempt to address the question of how sin, especially original sin, is possible on the account of the freedom presented in the first part of this book. I will begin with an account of what sin is. I will then integrate that account of sin into the classical Augustinian understanding of human moral psychology as it pertains to action. Having done this, I will first discuss the fall of Lucifer and his cohort and then apply this account to the fall of man. In anticipation of those who would reject this story as a mere fantasy, I propose to illustrate the effects of original sin as they display themselves in our disordered appetites, unruly passions, and inordinate desires. This will prepare us for the theological examination, in the next chapter, of the problem of grace and free will.

WHAT IS SIN?

To begin with, then, what is sin? First, it is more than just immorality as such. While every immoral act may be a sin, not all sins are immoral acts considered as such. For example, acts that may be indifferent in themselves, being neither morally required nor morally impermissible, such as mandatory church attendance, refraining from meat on certain days, or obedience to a religious superior, may become obligatory in such a way that they are sinful to omit. This holds despite the fact that these practices can change with time or be dispensed with altogether from one age to another. For example, years ago, Catholics were forbidden to eat meat on Fridays. After the Second Vatican Council, this obligation was relaxed and then finally lapsed through disuse except during Lent. Prior to that time, it was a sin to eat meat on Friday; afterwards, it was a matter of personal choice whether to do so. The claim here is not that it was *not* a sin to eat meat on Friday prior to that time and that, in abolishing this practice, the church was confirming this to be the case in the same way that, in abolishing slavery, the American government was recognizing that slavery was always morally wrong, even when it was legally practiced. Quite the contrary, those who ate meat on Friday prior to Vatican II sinned, despite the fact that the obligation was solely religious rather than moral in character, limited in time, and subject to change. Since acts morally indifferent in themselves can be sinful, immorality, understood as action contrary to the positive moral law as apprehended by a well-formed conscience, is therefore not essential to sin.

What is essential to sin is that it is the free and fully informed act of disobedience to the divine will, as expressed either in revelation or through God's appointed representatives on Earth. Since the moral law is obligatory (i.e., binding on us regardless of our desires or self-interest) solely through the will of God, all violations of the moral law are automatically sins as well.[1] However, they are not sins simply because they

---

1. I hope to discuss and defend the divine command theory of moral obligation (as opposed to the divine command theory of morality) elsewhere and to discuss the vexed question of whether or not God can dispense us from what would ordinarily be morally

are immoral acts, i.e., acts done contrary to the moral law. That a certain action constitutes a sin involves an added theological dimension to that act, i.e., its being decreed and imposed upon our wills by God. Conscience, which apprehends the natural moral law, is capable of correctly judging an act good or bad, right or wrong, virtuous or vicious in and of itself. Unaided reason is capable in principle of understanding why those actions are good or bad, right or wrong, virtuous or vicious from its understanding of what human nature is and what constitutes human flourishing. God has decreed that law and revealed it to us in the operation of conscience in order that we might flourish according to our nature, not merely as an arbitrary imposition. Further, even the imposition of acts indifferent in themselves is intended to conduct us to our last end, eternal life with God. That some action is a sin, however, is knowable only through the recognition that conscience is the voice of God and the apprehension of his will and command for us. The wrongness of sin resides in its refusal to acquiesce to the divine will: in short, sin is disobedience to God. This disobedience compounds the wrongness of the act and constitutes the lion's share of the evil that act represents. When that disobedience is deliberate, freely chosen, and fully informed, it is also culpable and deserving of punishment as its natural consequence.

Virtue, we are told, is its own reward. In a similar way, sin is its own punishment. What God has decreed for us is not arbitrary, but intended to lead us to eternal life with him. Sin, then, has the effect of leading us away from eternal life and cutting us off from God, earning for us eternal separation from him and the irrevocable loss of our ultimate felicity.[2] Further, when we sin, we do so through our own free choice, throwing away our only chance for lasting happiness. Because God has given us free will and respects our choices on that account, in allowing us to sin and reap the consequences of our own choices, God is not obliged to intervene and prevent us from doing so. The fault is our own, and the absolute innocence of God is preserved. Although God *antecedently* desires that all human beings be saved and could override our free will if he

---

required according to the natural law and to oblige us to do something contrary to that law and argue that he can, i.e., that the teleological suspension of the ethical is possible and sometimes even actual.

2. Universalists, of course, will disagree. Here I am following the mainstream Christian tradition, according to which not everyone will be saved. Although in principle universalism could be true, I think it is more likely that it is not. See Griffiths, *Problems of Religious Diversity*, 161–68, especially 161–63, on this point.

chose to do so, God's *consequent* will is that some should perish eternally for their sins in accordance with their own free choice. God's infallible foreknowledge of this outcome and tacit approval of it constitute his decree of predestination, reprobating those who resist him to the end. God, then, does not positively reprobate anyone; instead, he merely does not act to prevent the worst-case outcome, thereby merely permitting it to happen, rather than positively bringing it about. This, however, is to get ahead of ourselves; let us first consider the notion of sin in the context of the Christian Platonist moral psychology I have sketched elsewhere.

The Ontology of the Good

According to Christian neo-Platonism, God is both the ontic good and the exemplary good for all creatures. God is *Being Itself*, the ultimate reality expressing the fullness of being and thus the perfect being that expresses all the potentialities for existence-as-activity integrated in the highest and best way in a single substance.[3] In this way, then, God is also Goodness Itself, substantial good realized in a concrete individual entity. Every creature, however, simply by being, i.e., instantiating an essence in and by means of an individual act of existing, is (*eo ipso*) *a* being, an imperfect participation in what God fully realizes. Thus, merely for a thing to exist as *what* it is (instantiating its essence) *is* for it to be good so far forth. More than this, however, each thing, by realizing its essence, *participates* by imitation in the Good by *aspiring* to the perfection of being in a manner appropriate to its nature. In this way, God is also the exemplary good for every creature, though in a unique way for each. God, being infinitely participable by creatures, provides a unique exemplar for each kind of creature through his own essence as perfect being. In turn, creatures themselves are capable only of realizing their aspiration within the natural limits imposed upon them by their limited essences. Each creature inevitably falls infinitely short of the fullness of being as represented by God; as such, none achieves any material resemblance with God. Nevertheless, God is (to use Aristotelian terminology) the *final cause* to which all reality tends, drawing each thing to the fullest realization of being of which it is capable given its nature within the overall economy of the world order decreed by God to maximize this end overall.

---

3. Duncan, *Proof*, 151–65.

The next point to note is this: In creatures that possess and instantiate a characteristic pattern of development, the essence/nature of each dictates an end, purpose, work, operation, characteristic function, or optimal state that best executes and realizes that essence/nature. Each such being has, in virtue of its kind, a *telos* at which it aims and attempts to realize within the limits of the circumstances in which it finds itself. Given this, it is possible for us to specify what goodness/perfection for each kind of thing consists in by reference to its telos, which specifies what the thing is "good for." In turn, what is *good or bad for* that thing, i.e., objectively beneficial for or harmful to it, is in turn specifiable by reference to that same telos. Consideration of this brings us to the threshold of the question concerning good insofar as this is a matter of choice and action—the realm of ethics as such—but only to the threshold of that question. We must first consider the common biological foundation for the good in this sense that we share with other animals.

SENTIENCE AND MOTIVATION

The above account, as true as it is, nevertheless needs further specification. Inanimate beings, which are subject to natural processes but have no natural pattern of development as part of their nature, largely express their natures as completely as they are able by their mere constitution. Variations in the exercise of their capacities and powers are largely the consequence of external circumstances that are indifferent to the thing itself, e.g., a magnet will attract iron filings when they are present in its electromagnetic field; otherwise, the magnet will not. Simple living things like plants do exhibit basic life functions and instantiate a standard, specifiable pattern of growth, development, and decline like that we find in other living things, but without any apparent awareness of what is going on in the environment around them. Even so, it seems possible to make objective and correct judgments about what constitutes the good for, say, an African violet by reference to its optimal state of healthy reproductive maturity. Still, we do not find any more interesting insight into goodness for creatures such as ourselves until we consider the case of sentient beings, i.e., beings capable of conscious awareness of the world around them, interaction with that world, and recognition of how that interaction affects them for well or ill. We will consider the case of sentient, nonrational creatures first, although everything we say will apply, *mutatis mutandis*, to our own case.[4]

Sentient beings possess the capacity for conscious awareness, the power to feel, sense, and perceive the world around them. Although some animals are very primitive, have limited sense-modalities, and have little if any conscious experience, those animals naturally characterized by the sense of sight (even if this ability has atrophied through the influence of the environment, as in cave-dwelling salamanders) have very advanced sense-modalities. It is quite probable that they possess a contentful stream of consciousness of which they are aware at every waking moment. In virtue of this capacity for conscious awareness, such beings possess the powers to monitor their own bodily states and to perceive the world around them. The combination of these two powers makes it possible for them to engage in behavior relevant to and in some manner directed toward the achievement of their telos when taken in the context of their further ability for local motion. In this context, the sentient being's conscious awareness becomes related to external behavior in the form of *motivation*, classes of various kinds of feeling that evoke behavioral response to stimuli of various kinds. Although animals appear to have some limited capacity for learning from experience on an individual basis, by far the greater part of their behavior is genetically determined by inherited tropisms and instincts that belong to the species due to the course of its biological evolution.

Appetite

For creatures of this sort, the most common and pressing forms of motivation are those associated with a sentient being's capacity to consciously monitor its own inner states, which we associate with common, primitive appetites, such as the those for food, drink, warmth and, when triggered by appropriate conditions, sexual activity. In each case, the appetite in question is aroused by a physiological mechanism that produces discomfort in the face of hunger, thirst, cold, or an appropriate mate that motivates that being to behave in such a way as to relieve that discomfort. Appetites of the sort we are concerned with here are associated with various spontaneously occurring feelings, such as hunger, thirst, coldness, and sexual arousal. These feelings are powerful, unpleasant and, as

---

4. This, of course, can only be a sketch of the full view, which I hope to present elsewhere.

time goes on, increasingly urgent; however, they are not intentional in any sense. They neither reveal their causes nor portend that which will relieve them, so that an animal caught in their grips must cast around in the environment for something that will serve the turn. In the case of nonhuman animals, instinct has evolved in such a way that they are, for the most part, automatically led to whatever it is that will relieve the appetite. With regard to appetite, the optimal state is one of homeostatic equilibrium, or "zero need," and the acquisition of the object that relieves hunger, thirst, etc., restores that state of appetitive "rest."

Desire

Human beings have the same appetites as other animals and some instinctual guidance in discovering the objects that will relieve them and restore the state of zero need. However, being rational, human beings are also capable of grasping both the causes of their appetites and of discovering their objects, thus arriving at objective, self-conscious awareness of both their current state and the object that will satisfy it. At this point, a new factor enters human motivation—the element of *desire*. Unlike mere appetite considered as such, desire is cognitive and intentional: it is always "desire *for*" and specified by its object. Desires, unlike appetites, do not normally arise spontaneously, but they do arise in the course of experience. Desire is also a state of deprivation that seeks its completion in the acquisition and enjoyment of the desired object. Desire is thus cognitive in two senses. First, desire is cognitive inasmuch as experience and contemplation of the object precedes the production of the desire for that object; desire is thus *mediated by knowledge* and thus normally an occurrent mental state.[5] Second, it is cognitive in that it is directed on an object that the desirer *judged* to be desirable, a mental act possible only for a self-conscious subject possessing a concept of the good. Although nonhuman animals do possess the ability to acquire certain habits of pursuit-behavior that we ordinarily describe using the language of desire, to the extent that animals are nonrational, this sort of language has to be regarded as analogical rather than univocal when applied to them.

Sorting this out requires that we briefly consider the relation between desire on the one hand and pleasure and pain on the other. The matter is more complicated than many philosophers suppose it to

---

5. There is no space here to discuss the notions of repressed, or unconscious, desires made so popular by Freud.

be. First, we need to distinguish what we might call *sensual* pleasure and pain from *desiderative* pleasure and pain properly so called. It is a physiological fact that there exist pain-producing mechanisms in the body, including afferent (i.e., pain-producing) nerves, which inform us of bodily damage, stress, injury, and illness. Pains of this sort occur unbidden, spontaneously motivating avoidance behavior with regard to their perceived causes. There also appears to be a "pleasure center" in the mammalian brain that can be stimulated by various activities, especially those naturally associated with the gratification of natural appetite. As Plato noted, the pleasure associated with eating, drinking, sex, etc., is coterminous with the pain it relieves, so that once the pain of deprivation is relieved, the pleasure associated with that activity ceases as well.[6] For this reason, these appetites in nonhuman animals are generally regulated: animals eat when hungry, drink when thirsty, pursue sexual activity when stimulated by pheromones or other external triggers of sexual appetite, and are otherwise not bothered by those appetites. As such, their appetites generally serve the overall economy of their health, well-being, and species survival as expressed in the realization of their essence.

For cognitive beings possessing the capacity for desire, however, the experience of the sensual pleasure associated with the gratification of appetite can become an object of desire in its own right. One can come to desire the experience of the sensual pleasure produced by the pleasure center as an end-in-itself and thus devise means to stimulate the appetite *artificially* in order to enjoy sensual pleasure more often.[7] In the same way, we discover that there are ways to stimulate directly the pleasure center using both naturally occurring and artificially concocted chemical substances, thus achieving the enjoyment of sensuous pleasure for its own sake. Thus, the use of tobacco, alcohol, cannabis, LSD, methamphetamine, and so on in the pursuit of an induced "high" is quite common among human beings.[8] Such behavior, unless carefully controlled, is usually physically and psychologically addictive and, in the course of time, is accompanied by tremendous pain and stress resulting from physical addiction. In order to avoid the pain of deprivation,

---

6. *Gorgias*, S495–97.

7. As in, e.g., the use of pornography to stimulate one's sexual appetite in the absence of its normally appropriate object, something only human beings can engage in.

8. Some animals do this as well, though apparently simply through accident.

the addict is forced to devote an inordinate amount of time, effort, and resources to the pursuit of sensuous pleasure, undermining both health and character and leading in extreme cases to criminality, madness, and death. To say the least, addiction of this sort is deleterious to the pursuit of human flourishing; sensuous pleasure should never be pursued for its own sake or as an end in itself.[9]

The second sort of pleasure and pain that concerns us here is wholly psychological, rather than based in human physiology as such. This is the pleasure and pain associated with desire satisfaction and desire frustration. Desire is a major source of the psychological motivation, inciting us to act in pursuit of an object judged by an agent to be desirable. Some desires are mild and can be easily ignored, others stronger and accompanied by a sense of urgency or a conviction that one cannot be happy unless one acquires the object that one wants. Very often, unrequited desire of this sort is perceived as extremely painful in a psychological sense, even though not accompanied by physical pain; such permanently unrequited desire can blight one's entire life unless one can manage to "get over it."

Similarly, there is pleasure that accompanies the initial satisfaction of any desire simply due to my getting what I want. This pleasure is often short-lived, as when based on a limited perspective of which I am quickly disabused; on other occasions, my desires change so that what I thought I wanted desperately at some earlier time means nothing to me when I finally achieve or acquire it. This pleasure is also an indirect object of pursuit, as Aristotle among others has noted.[10] It is only because I value the object of the desire *as such* that I am capable of desiring it and thus taking desiderative pleasure in the acquisition and enjoyment of the object. Unless I desire things for reasons independent of their status as being objects of desire, they cannot be such objects for me; a person who desired nothing but pleasure in that sense could never attain his or her goal. As such, the pleasure associated with desire satisfaction can never be an end in itself.

---

9. This is not to claim that sensuous pleasure should never be pursued. See Duncan, *Primer*, 20–23. In this early book, I suggest that limited indulgence in what I there call "the pleasures of the flesh" can be redeemed through being integrated into the pursuit of an intrinsic good.

10. NE 1174b14–1175a3.

Passion

Passion and emotion are likewise cognitive, involving belief and judgment in relation to the object of desire. However, unlike the case of desire, which concerns the desired object as to be pursued, acquired and enjoyed, passion and emotion are subsequent to this and focused on the object as being currently possessed and enjoyed by the agent. Passion is reflected in our reactions to perceived threat to or loss of those things that we regard as essential to our current happiness. Some of these emotions are focused primarily on ourselves, such as joy, fear, anger, jealousy, envy, shame, and grief. Others, such as sympathy, compassion, pity, and agapeistic love, are focused on others as we see them related to ourselves, either through empathetic sharing in their plight or through sentimental identification with them. In every case, emotions have to do with the good we believe ourselves to possess and retain as a necessary component of our happiness.

Others have made these points. What is not so frequently noted—and when noted, most often hotly denied—by philosophical writers on emotion is that, despite their cognitive content, emotions are constituted by strong feelings that assault us as though from without, inciting us to overt behavior expressive of those feelings. Emotions as such have no objects, though they are evoked by judgments concerning objects; they "desire" only their own expression in some form that discharges that energy and relieves its felt pressure. In certain primitive emotions that seem continuous with the "fight" and "flight" reactions we instinctively share with nonrational animals, there are certain stereotypical behaviors that relevantly express and discharge the emotional energy—the deer sees a predator and runs away, the cornered rat bares its teeth and prepares to attack. In human beings, however, a much wider range of threats, irritants, and acquaintance with our own problems and those of others is to be found. In many instances, no relevant behavior will do anything to alter or improve the situation. Our emotional upset, however, is still present, leading us to "act out" in any manner that allows us to "feel better," if even for a moment. I am clumsy with my coffee and spilling some on my hand, burn myself; suddenly angry, I throw my coffee cup against the wall, breaking it and making a huge mess as coffee splashes all over the room. My anger is now dissipated, soon to be replaced by feelings of rueful foolishness and guilt at my lack of self-control. Regardless, in this context the point is this: There is no requirement that there be a direct relation of relevance between the cause of one's emotional state, one's current situation, and the behavior by means of which one expresses that state and discharges the emotional energy. Passion is thus an essentially nonrational source of motivation, requiring the external control of dispassionate reason in order to prevent the worst consequences that can result from acting as it prompts us.

There is much more to be said about the nature of human motivation. However, this will have to do for our purposes here. Let us now return to our main topic, the nature of the good for the human person.

REASON, MOTIVATION AND THE GOOD

Rational beings possess a concept of *the good* as the *objectively* desirable. The good considered as such is the object of all motivation, whether instinctual/appetitive, passional, or in the form of specific occurrent desires. We are "hard-wired" to pursue the good, which appears to us under many guises. However, rational beings neither directly apprehend nor instinctively acquire the good as such. Our apprehension of the good as such is always mediated by our apprehension of individual, concrete goods that cannot be sensibly identified with the full, total, and complete good. Those we are aware of are always only limited goods, which are just one among many others. The good as such, therefore, would have to be some combination of these. Initially, however, the goods that present themselves to us in experience have to be the starting point for the pursuit of the good itself or as such. Elsewhere I have attempted to work this out along lines suggested by Grisez and Finnis.[11] Here I want to concentrate on finite goods as objects of rational free choice.

Ideally, our occurrent appetites, passions, and desires would be strong presumptive evidence for the objective goodness of those finite goods we apprehend. Even at best, though, such a presumption would be a defeasible one. The pursuit of the good, then, requires the cooperation of reason, which critically examines the putative good in order to judge whether it is as it appears. Furthermore, many different and competing things strike us as good, not all of which are mutually compatible. Choices must therefore be made, and it will not do to make these choices haphazardly or simply on the basis of the whim of the moment. Deliberation and rational choice are required if we are to attain the

---

11. Duncan, *Primer*, chapter 2.

objective good for the person and thus human flourishing, the optimal expression of our common human nature given our individual endowments, conditions, and circumstances. The rational, judicious exercise of our free will is necessary for this; without it, we can have no hope of achieving *eudaimonia*, or objective happiness. Elsewhere I have tried to explain how it is that a combination of experience and rational reflection makes moral knowledge possible for us.[12] Here I will simply assume that it is possible for us to acquire this knowledge in fact. I now wish to develop this conception from an Augustinian perspective.

Let us begin with the notion of the *human motivational structure*, what Socrates meant by "soul" used in the nonreligious sense. The human motivational structure will be a complex collection of appetites, passions, desires, habits, moods, tendencies, and character traits possessing various degrees of felt strength and integration into our overall personalities. This motivational structure will be partially constitutive of our worldview, as well as the foundation for our philosophy of life, the expression of that worldview in attitude, speech, and action.[13] Like one's merely inchoate or implicit worldview itself, it will be a haphazard, largely fluid collection of various contending influences, impulses, and energies possessing an equally haphazard structure. However, the possibility of attaining the good as such requires that the soul in this sense be *properly structured* and thus attain that structure if it does not possess it already.

Plato presented a famous analysis of the parts of the soul and their proper hierarchical alignment that is still sound today and relevant to our present inquiry. The first part of the soul is *reason*, whose proper object is *knowledge* and the perfection of which is *wisdom*. The second, the *spirited* part of the soul, is the principle of our self-image and sense of honor and thus of the passions as well, whose object is *approval, respect,* and *honor*, both in our own case and that of other rational beings. The third part of the soul, the *appetitive* part, produces sensual motivation and spontaneous, first-order desires for the things of this world formed in response to experience and has pleasure (both sensual and in the form of desire-satisfaction) as its object. As we all know, Plato asserts that the proper order of the parts of the soul results from the joint action of rea-

---

12. Duncan, *Primer*, 55–76.

13. Duncan, *Being, Truth, and Knowledge*, chapter 1. Here I have discussed the concept of a worldview and the role it plays in philosophy; I hope to revise this discussion elsewhere.

son and the spirited part ruling over the appetitive part and controlling it in accordance with the dictates of reason. Since only knowledge can conduct us to the objective good, reason must take the lead in directing us to eudaimonia. However, reason cannot succeed in doing this unless I am committed at a deep level to this project, identify myself with it, and judge myself by the ideal that the pursuit of the objective good dictates for the human person. This will be the case only if my image of myself and sense of honor are firmly tied up with that ideal such that to betray it for mere fleeting pleasure is literally to betray and debase myself. Only then will my pursuit of and indulgence in sensual pleasure and the pursuit of material things be moderated in accordance with the requirements of right reason. As Socrates, Plato, and Aristotle classically understood this, the key to this transformation is the cultivation of the virtues, especially the four cardinal virtues: prudence, temperance, courage/fortitude, and justice.

From the perspective of Christian theology, Augustine of Hippo transforms this theoretical construct and its project by translating its teachings in light of a phenomenology of *love*. My current motivational structure reflects the differential love I bear to the various objects that attract it. Some I love more and thus am more strongly attracted to, whereas others I love less and pursue less ardently. As such: *amor meus, pondus meum*—my love is my weight. What sort of person I am depends not on what I say or think about myself or pay lip service to, but instead on how I feel about things and express those feelings in my externally observable "pursuit behavior." What I truly want is expressed in what I actively seek after and attempt to acquire and enjoy for myself. Augustine retains part of the classical tradition by supposing that there is a normative, hierarchical ordering of the available objects of love expressible in terms of the neo-Platonic account of the good sketched earlier. Things are to be loved in accordance with their objective value (or ontic good) dictating their relative desirability with regard to each other. A later Christian thinker, Jonathan Edwards, calls this *true virtue* expressed as "benevolence to being."[14]

Understood in these terms, Augustinians maintain that reason dictates that our motivational structure should mirror reality and that our motivating loves should correspond to the hierarchy of objective values that structures the universe of being. For our purposes here, we can consider just the four following classes of things: God, the self, other

---

14. Edwards, *Freedom of the Will*, 14–41.

persons, and material goods. Reason, expressed as benevolence toward being, dictates that we should love things in proportion to their objective value or being. As such, God is to be loved above all things, because God is Being and Goodness Itself, the perfect realization of existence-as-activity. Since human beings are made in the image and likeness of God due to their possessing intellect and free will, it is also appropriate for us to love them as well; thus, we are bidden to love ourselves for our own sakes and our neighbor as ourselves, hence as ends-in-themselves. By contrast, since material possessions exist, not as ends-in-themselves but only as means to other ends, they are to be loved less than God or persons and never pursued for their own sakes, but only as means to the end of human flourishing.

Since this is the dictate of reason as understood in the context of the neo-Platonic theory of value, the well-ordered soul seeks first the things of God, then the well-being of persons, both oneself and others, then material possessions and comforts and only to the degree that these genuinely subserve the end of human flourishing. The presence of the right order of the soul will be reflected not merely in one's outward speech, behavior, and lifestyle, but also in one's inner life, including one's very feelings, appetites, desires, and passions. Benevolence to being, then, is no mere matter of obedience to law or external conformity to moral and religious requirements imposed from without. To the contrary, it is the genuine expression of one's whole being and structures one's entire personality. One is not merely acting as reason dictates or morality requires, but instead simply as one's predominant love spontaneously prompts one to do. This is how we ought to understand St. Paul's admonition to love God and do what one will. In that case, one acts from love of God and, in so doing, effortlessly fulfills the requirements of reason; one is led by feeling but judges in accordance with what reason approves.

Sin and Sinfulness

Sin is a positive act that in many cases actualizes moral evil, pain, and suffering in the world. It is therefore difficult at first glance to understand the Christian Platonist conviction that sin is not genuinely real but only the consequence of the privation of the good. The foregoing account, however, helps us to understand how this claim can be true. Just as right action flows effortlessly from the well-ordered soul animated by benevolence toward being, characterized by love of God before all things, so too does sin flow from sinfulness, the privation of the ontic good in the human soul. A soul that lacks the proper order dictated by reason will *ipso facto* be a disordered soul, one in which the right ordering of the parts of the soul will be absent and some other ordering contrary to right reason will prevail. In turn, such a soul will love those things of which it is aware in an improper way, loving some things more than their objective value warrants and others less than they ought. This, in turn, will be reflected in one's feelings, appetites, desires, and passions and externalized in the behavior to which those impulses prompt us. To do what reason and morality require will be difficult, unpleasant, and burdensome; one may externally conform to what morality and religion require, but one does not really want to do so "inside" and will look for opportunities to shirk. More often than not, one will fail to do what reason requires and instead pursue what one really loves in preference to it.

In theological terms, this lack of the proper ordering of the parts of the soul resulting in disordered and improper love we call "*sinfulness*." Sinfulness is the cause of actual sin but is itself merely the privation of the good that belongs to the soul by nature, i.e., the proper ordering among its "loves." Though the effects of sinfulness are real and destructive of the self, others, and reality in general, it remains that sinfulness itself is not a positive reality, but instead only a privation, the lack of the *ontic* good of the soul. Moral evil, then, is the consequence of ontic evil, which is always a privation of the good and never a positive reality in its own right. To the extent that anything *is*, it is good by that very fact. A thing is bad or evil only by failing to be what its nature dictates that it ought to be in ideal terms, i.e., by failing to exemplify its nature optimally as dictated by its telos.

In turn, this state constitutes the flourishing of that thing in accordance with its nature. In rational beings, this state of flourishing also constitutes eudaimonia, objective happiness. In Christian tradition, that state of happiness is oneness with God, something experienced to some extent in this life by holy, saintly people but which can be enjoyed in its fullness only in the *visio beatifica* of the next life in which, as St. Paul puts it, we will see God face to face.[15] Considered simply as biological entities, human beings share the same end, or telos, as other animals, i.e., the attainment of reproductive maturity. As rational beings possessing intellect and will, we are called to the full development and enjoyment

---

15. Kirk, *Vision of God*, especially 379–94.

of our powers of theoretical, practical, and technical reason and through them, a life of participation in the intrinsic goods to which that nature directs us.[16] In addition, the Christian religion contends that there is another, supernatural end for human beings continuous with and capable of completing our nature; this end is nothing else but God himself and eternal life with him in paradise.

Sinfulness, the lack of the proper ordering of the parts of the soul, makes the pursuit of eudaimonia and the attainment of our last end impossible. We are unable to love God above all things unless our souls are properly ordered. Even if in our lucid moments we can recognize the demands of reason and muster a wistful regret that we are incapable of doing that which we can see, on balance, to be objectively desirable for us, we cannot even genuinely desire to do so. A drug addict can judge that his addiction is not desirable from the rational point of view yet still desire to take the drug due to the influence of his physical addiction and desire this more than being cured of his addiction. In like manner, a sinner can judge rationally that his or her sin is incompatible with the attainment of true happiness (and thus on some level desire not to sin) yet be quite helpless to change his or her ways because the desire for sin and its objects is too strong to resist. To be in a state of sin, then, is to exemplify both cognitive and practical irrationality. Such a condition, when reflected upon, is bound to produce feelings of guilt, self-loathing, and helplessness—as Paul puts it, "the good I would do I do not, and the evil I would not do, that I do."[17] All too many people (especially nowadays) attempt to eliminate this state of cognitive dissonance by refusing to acknowledge their sinfulness and attempting to persuade themselves that there is no such thing as God or sin, and that in doing whatever they want to do, they are doing nothing wrong, at least as long as "no one gets hurt." If the claims of the Christian religion are true, however, they are only fooling themselves.

Positive acts of sin follow upon sinfulness as the privation of the proper order of the parts of the soul. Sin reflects the motivational structure that produces it and its dominant loves, whether it is sensual pleasure, power over others, material possessions, wealth for its own sake, fame, or some combination of these—the list goes on. Sinfulness also is reflected in our feelings, passions, and emotions as these structure our

16. Duncan, *Primer*, chapters 1–3.
17. Rom 7:15.

reactions to what happens around us. Sin is not aberrant or a merely accidental accretion on one's true self; for the sinner, it is the expression of one's true self and a consequence of following one's natural bent. For the person afflicted with a disordered motivational structure, not to sin is contrary to his or her nature, and sin can be avoided only with discomfort and duress. Not even fear of punishment or other loss can be counted upon to dissuade the sinner from expressing his or her inner self. Despite one's best efforts, one's sinfulness will express itself in the form of wicked, immoral, irreligious, and harmful acts of all sorts, all flowing from the fundamental privation of a rightly ordered soul.

HOW SIN IS POSSIBLE

There is a well-known paradox concerning the possibility of sin understood as the product of free choice. On the one hand, for us to sin requires that we knowingly and willingly choose the lesser in preference to the greater good. Supposing that we are already sinful, there is no great mystery about this; our disordered motivational structure distorts the objects of our love in such a way as to make the lesser good appear to be the greater one. So, in knowingly and willingly choosing against the dictates of reason, we are helped by the fact that we feel the attraction of the lesser good more keenly than the greater good that reason approves and thus find it is easy to choose the former in preference to the latter. This does not excuse us, of course, because we know that in so choosing we are doing wrong, giving in to temptation by following our natural bent, itself distorted by our individual sinfulness. However, the mystery of sin concerns how sin is possible in the first place. Presumably, God initially created his free, rational creatures in such a manner that their souls were rightly ordered, as the Garden of Eden story in Genesis naturally suggests.[18] For such beings, the objectively grounded relative values of things would have been clearly apprehended and our natural inclinations perfectly aligned to that apprehension. In such case, it is difficult to see how sin would even be possible through a free choice of the will.

---

18. God could hardly be loving and benevolent if he created us in a defective manner that would ensure that we would sin. Further, in such case, that we should sin would evidently be God's will, and thus in sinning we would be doing no more than fulfilling God's will, something for which we can hardly be held blameworthy or liable to punishment. Not so, say the supralapsarians, but there is no room to consider their views here.

What possible incentive would anyone have to sin in such circumstances? On the other hand, if sin was not possible in this original, pristine state, then either our first parents never sinned, or they were caused to sin by some invasive force that overrode reason and their prelapsarian natural bent in such a way as to cause them to sin contrary to their will. The first case seems obviously contrary to fact.[19] The second would make sin both causally determined and discontinuous with our personality and thus not something for which we could be held responsible. It seems, then, that we face a tripartite dilemma.[20] If we were made to sin by being created sinful, i.e., with a defective motivational structure, not only would God be complicit in our sinning, but it would also be the case that we could not have done otherwise and so could not be justly punished for our sins. Alternatively, if we were caused to sin by forces outside of our control that overrode our original innocence by *force majeur*, we did not do so freely and thus did not meet the necessary condition for being in sin as defined above. Lastly, if we were created in a state of original innocence, it seems unaccountable that we could have ever sinned at all. Yet most Christians hold that Scripture reveals that sin is real and that there were at least two cases of "original sin," involving the fall of the bad angels and the fall of Adam and Eve, our first ancestors, from a state of original innocence to one characterized by irremediable sinfulness.[21] It seems that Christians have no choice and must embrace the mystery: rational beings freely sinned despite being in a state of original innocence in which there was no innate tendency or motivation to sin.

The account of free will sketched in the first part of this book suggests a way in which we can glean at least a partial understanding of how this sort of sin—traditionally called "original sin"—is possible. As we saw earlier, acts of free choice are the result of immanent mental acts by

---

19. See below 93–95.

20. That's right. The solecisms "trilemma" and "quadrilemma" (etc.) are the product of false etymology; a dilemma is merely any division of alternatives, without regard to number.

21. I have no interest here in debating the details of these stories or the degree of literality with which they ought to be invested. Further, a number of theologians, beginning with St. Irenaeus and including such twentieth-century notables as Teilhard de Chardin and John Hick, have suggested that the Fall was a necessary loss of innocence that constitutes a "fall upward" rather than deviation from God's original intention. I believe that these proposals are orthodox and have merit; however, I will not adopt or explore them here.

means of which we control the direction of our attention and thus the structure of our mental life by choosing to attend to some things rather than others. We can accomplish this in either of two ways. First, *non-precisively*, as when I shift background and foreground in consciousness, concentrating first on one aspect of something, then on another, bringing each in turn into centrality in my intentional field of consciousness. The other way is by means of *precisive* abstraction, in which I cease attending to some of the elements of my intentional field of consciousness in order to concentrate on others in isolation from the usual context in which they are embedded. It is this device, by means of which I cease thinking about some of my mental contents, that I use to freely constitute one of a set of alternatives as the object of my choice, thus allowing it to proceed through consciousness to enactment. The same device, I wish to suggest, explains how original sin might have come about.

In *The Silmarillion*, J. J. R. Tolkien presents a thinly disguised allegory for the fall of Satan in his story about how Melkor, brightest of the *ainur* (angels), becomes the enemy of good and light. When God creates the world, he first creates the ainur and teaches them to sing, first as individuals, then in small groups, then as a celestial chorus. Melkor begins as a member of the heavenly choir responsible, through its song, for the creation of the cosmic order. At first, he concentrates on singing in such a way as to carry his part in the choir, blending with the other voices. Then, one day, he begins to listen to his own voice, which is, in fact, the most beautiful of all those in the chorus. As he continues to listen to it, he ceases to listen to the rest of the choir and at last cares for nothing but what shows off his voice to best effect. He begins to ornament and vary on the rhythm and harmony of the song until at last he ruins both with his innovations, all of which are born of the desire to highlight the beauty of his individual voice.[22] By so doing, he also ruins the emerging world of which the song is the medium of creation. Eventually, the supreme being of the Silmarillion is able to weave his discordant song into a greater melody and thus overcome the damage that Melkor has done, bringing good out of evil and redeeming even Melkor's errors in the end. In the meantime, however, Melkor becomes the implacable enemy of light and the lord of darkness.

This, of course, is only a myth and a literary myth at that. Nevertheless, it suggests a way in which the foregoing account of free

22. Tolkien, *Silmarillion*, first section "Music of the Ainur."

will could explain how original sin is possible. By means of precisive abstraction, it is possible for us to isolate an element of the contents of consciousness and dwell on it in isolation from its usual context. We can constitute a sense-datum, such as a sensation of redness, and treat it as the sole subject of conscious awareness, even though we never ordinarily experience a red-sense datum except as a perceptible quality of a putatively external body, integrated with other such qualities in a single sense experience, such as seeing a ball. There is generally no problem with this, since only philosophers and introspective psychologists are likely to perform such a mental operation. To do so, however, is nonetheless to create a kind of self-generated illusion that distorts the reality of redness as an object of experience. If we forget that our own mental act of precisive abstraction creates the distinct sense-datum "redness" in isolation from its context in ordinary experience, it becomes very easy to fall into empiricism, phenomenalism, Kantian constructivism, or associationism. These views all share the same error, inasmuch as each takes mental *disjecta membra* (such as sense-data) and supposes them to be original, self-existing atoms of consciousness, which are somehow combined by the mind to create objects of awareness. The philosophical consequences of this error are too well known by now to be in serious doubt.[23] Yet it arises from our having forgotten that what was simply the product of our own mental activity is only that and in no way real apart from it, resulting in one's mistaking the product of that activity for its cause.

The same, I suggest, applies in the case of sin. By means of an act of precisive abstraction, we constitute a lesser good in such a way that its status with regard to the greater good is ignored or left out of the picture. We thus create the illusion that this good is the only (or the greater) good in the circumstances. This is only an illusion, of course, but if we continue to dwell on that illusion, it becomes possible for us to deceive ourselves into thinking that this is not so, but instead the truth of things. The more we dwell on our own fantasies, the more we love them and the more attached we become to them, so that we cannot bear to give them up. On one level, we know that they are false and merely the invention of our own fancy; on another, we desire them to be true despite that fact, so we create a self-generated state of "forgetting" that gratifies that desire

---

23. Of course, I don't expect empiricists et al. to agree with this. They will insist that sense-data are the products of the analysis of our mental life, not merely created by an act of precisive abstraction. I hope to argue this at length in another place.

for us.[24] This allows us to "live" the illusion that has become so important to us, generally to our cost.

It is often said that pride is the root cause of sin, and so it is in a way. However, since pride is itself a mode of sinfulness, it cannot be understood to be the literal cause of sin as such. However, the mechanism I have just described does explain how this sort of pride as the root of sin can arise. Melkor listens to his own voice and finds it beautiful, and it is. It is not as beautiful as the combined voices of the heavenly choir taken as a whole, but it is beautiful nevertheless and, indeed, the most beautiful of the voices created by God. By choosing to concentrate only on his own voice, Melkor is able to appreciate its beauty and to love it on that account, but by continually dwelling on its beauty, he allows himself to forget that its beauty is not for its own sake, but rather for its contribution to the beauty of the choir as a whole. Melkor thus begins to see his singing as an end in itself and as more important than that of the choir as a whole.[25] This is false and the freely chosen, self-imposed, misconstrual of the true nature of the situation as understood by reason. At the same time, it is not at all difficult to see how it could arise, even though it is not motivated by any originally sinful motive or tendency.

More generally, we can give the following account. The good of any created being is derivative from that of God, its creator, and while inherent and intrinsic to it (at least insofar as it is objectively constituted there), nevertheless this good pales in significance to that of the Source of which it is merely the crepuscular reflection. The notion of an inherent and *underived* value existing in any creature is an illusion, and this includes the intrinsic value of persons as well. To constitute oneself as *autonomous*, as existing independently of God, and as existing as an end-in-oneself as over against him, can be accomplished by means of the act of precisive abstraction I have detailed above. From this perspective, I exist as an end-in-myself, not simply by reference to other persons (who therefore owe me certain prerogatives) but *simpliciter*. This is, of course, utterly false if theism is true but, despite that, something all too easy for us to convince ourselves is true. If we dwell long and hard on this picture of things and begin to love ourselves for our own sakes alone with-

---

24. See Fingarette, *Self-Deception*, 111–50, on this point.

25. Anyone who has ever sung in a choir (as I have) will have experienced this phenomenon; indeed, there is hardly a singer anywhere who is not guilty of Melkor's illusion, including me.

out reference to the Source of all that in us is worth loving, it is precisely in this way that the sin of pride, the root of all other forms of sinfulness, can arise. If this pride becomes habitual, then we progressively lose the ability to recover the original, rational point of view that we freely abandoned in order to indulge in the fantasy from which pride arises. It therefore becomes endemic to our character, subsequently structures our desires and passions, and through them structures our behavior as well.

In the same way, all sin in general requires that we create for ourselves the illusion that the lesser good is preferable to the greater good. The same mechanism, involving our power of abstraction, makes this possible in every case. We focus on some chosen object removed from its ordinary context, thus magnifying its apparent good, or we use non-precisive abstraction to highlight the positive features of some created good (bringing them into the foreground of consciousness) and to downplay its negative aspects (which recede into the background). This will be especially effective if those negative aspects or consequences are removed from us in time, less than absolutely certain or in any other way remote from our present situation or concerns. This again is a self-created illusion and need not fool us. However, if we dwell on it and come to prefer the illusion to the reality, we can thereby persuade ourselves that it is true or, at any rate, that we prefer it to the true and the real and will live and act as though it were, living in a state of willful self-deception. Thus, sinfulness of the sort associated with the fall of the bad angels and of the human race need not require some prior evil choice or inclination. It can be the result of an innocent or even random act of precisive or non-precisive abstraction that we continue to sustain in being and dwell on until we persuade ourselves that it is better than what, at another level, we know to be truly good and thus manage to deceive ourselves about. When this happens, our choice to act as though that illusion were true, i.e., to act as it prompts us, leads us into actual sin. Having explained how original sin is possible to begin with, let us now consider sin as it troubles the human condition.

ORIGINAL SINFULNESS AND ACTUAL SIN

The mainstream Judeo-Christian tradition authoritatively teaches that human beings were made in a state of original sinlessness, without any innate tendency to go wrong, and lived in an optimal environment in which no more was required in order for them to attain their full flourishing and supernatural end than to follow their natural bent. Nevertheless, they freely chose to turn away from God, the good, and reason and thus fell through their own fault. Because of this, they were denied the vision of God and declined into a state of permanent and irremediable sinfulness. Having explained how this is possible in principle in the previous section, we will not here trouble ourselves about the details of how this sad state of affairs came about.[26] We are in this context concerned with the aftermath of this decline.

The upshot is this: Due to original sin, human beings come into this world with an already disordered motivational system characterized by a natural bent that is contrary to what reason clearly apprehends to be the true and the good. As such, human beings naturally (i.e., spontaneously) desire what is contrary to their nature understood in the normative sense. Reason tells us that we ought to love God above all things, our neighbor as ourselves, and ourselves above the things of this world: wealth, fame, honor, and material possessions. It does not take much knowledge of this world or of human beings to discover exactly the opposite to be the case. How many of us risk our lives and our health in order to make more money so that we can afford luxury goods? How many of us really regard the needs and flourishing of others to be as important as our own? Who, beyond a few saintly persons, really love God to the point that they put him at the center of their lives? Exaggerated appetites, unruly passions, and disordered desires that even we can sometimes see to be inappropriate and harmful, both to others and to ourselves, plague all of us. We put up with and excuse our own faults as well as those of our friends and family, while we are less tolerant of those more distant from us. We do the best we can to tell ourselves that we are "all right" after all, or at any rate, not as bad as we could be. In this way, we avoid having to face ourselves as we really are.

26. There are a couple of different theories about how original sin came to be established as a permanent feature of the human soul. One theory is that Adam's sin directly corrupted his nature somehow and led to his passing this corrupted nature on to his offspring. Another is that God simply removed some preternatural gifts from Adam necessary for him to attain his supernatural end, and these being removed, made it impossible for him even to attain natural felicity. I am unable to discern which of these theories might be true; what I say here should be compatible with either of them. In any case, I reject the contention that we inherit not just original sin but the guilt for original sin, such that we are all born worthy of eternal punishment in hell. One can only be held liable for punishment for one's own sin, not those committed by others before we were born.

Since sinfulness is our unnatural natural condition, we are overwhelmingly attracted to the sinful actions that are expressive of our fallen nature. When we succumb to those temptations, we commit actual sins for which we are liable for punishment if those sins are not forgiven by God. All human beings over the age of reason are actual sinners and deserve divine punishment as a result; the natural bent of our nature is too hard for us to resist or to change on our own. However, this does not prevent our actual sins from being freely chosen and thus something for which we are rightly held responsible. While we cannot help sinning, given our disordered motivational structure, this does not mean that we are determined to commit any *particular* sin. On any occasion that we sin, we could have avoided that particular sin on that particular occasion. That sin is thus freely chosen because we could have done otherwise. As such, our responsibility for that sin is not mitigated by the fact that, given our nature, we cannot avoid sin altogether. Further, as we continue to commit sins, we begin to develop addictions, vices, and other sinful proclivities that become habitual. Ultimately, these are no longer resistible by the power of one's own will. However, given that these are the results of our initial free choices, we become responsible for the sins that flow from them as we commit them, even though we no longer have a free choice about the matter. No one, then, can claim that sin is not his or her fault, even if original sinfulness is not itself freely chosen.

Although we retain our free will and this arguably accounts for all of our actual sins, the "bentness" of our nature does not permit us freely to choose the good on a consistent basis, acquire virtue, or overcome our sinful condition through our own unaided efforts. Left to our own devices, it is impossible for us substantially to improve the human condition. Our best efforts are worthwhile and can make temporary improvements to human life over time. However, the dream of "perfecting human nature" through education, social reform, or institutional design, or through trusting in some sort of historical inevitability to save us in spite of ourselves is simply that. Nor can anyone attain true happiness or his/her end as a rational and spiritual being as long as we are burdened with sin. Things will never get much better, and they may get a lot worse, as long as we are left to ourselves.

The Christian message, however, is that we have not been left to ourselves. Although the fall of the human race and all its attendant sufferings and inconveniences are the result of original sin, and all of our sins are freely chosen, thus our own fault, God has not abandoned us. Despite having neither an obligation nor any need to do so, God lovingly and graciously offers us, through the atoning death of Jesus Christ, the means by which we can achieve both happiness and our last end. However, that is the rest of the story, to be told in the next two chapters.

5

Grace and Free Will

ELECTION, REPROBATION, AND THE JUSTICE OF ETERNAL PUNISHMENT

THE PROBLEM OF THE relation between grace and human free will is one of the most vexed questions in post-Reformation theology, one bound to evoke strong feelings, endless pamphlet wars, and accusations of heresy. Sects, denominations, and individual theologians have entrenched views on this topic, and nothing that anyone says is likely to shift their opinions. Furthermore, there is no point in addressing what follows to disinterested persons, since no one is likely even to investigate this question unless he or she is already interested, which interest most likely results from antecedent commitment to some view received by faith on the basis of religious authority. In presenting my own position on this issue, I do not expect that I will resolve all the issues to everyone's satisfaction or create some sort of breakthrough in our understanding of these issues. My reading of Protestant theologians, especially in the Reformed tradition, persuades me that this *cannot be done*, since many of them will not be satisfied with anything less than theological determinism as a condition of divine sovereignty.[1] However, I believe that the theory I will be putting forth here counts as orthodox within the boundaries of traditional Catholic theology. I claim no more for it than that.

I will begin by formulating the problem as I see it; in philosophy and theology, this is often half the battle by itself. My way of formu-

---

1. Of course, there is also the vibrant Arminian tradition within Protestantism that rejects theological determinism, and many of these theologians may find this view, or elements of it, to be useful in their own project of articulating the relation between grace and free will. In Protestant terms, I am a straightforward Arminian.

lating the problem may not meet with the approval of everyone, but it does seem to me to get at the root of the mystery of salvation insofar as grace is involved. I then attempt to explain how salvation can be wholly the work of grace and damnation solely the work of the human will by arguing that there is an asymmetry between how free will operates with regard to the acceptance of grace and its rejection.[2] In this way, I hope to avoid the extremes of theological determinism on the one hand and Pelagianism and semi-Pelagianism on the other.[3] The view that I defend will be a version of what Protestants call "Arminianism"; however, Catholic theologians have held similar views.[4] With these preliminaries out of the way, let us turn to the substantive account I will propose.

WHAT IS THE QUESTION CONCERNING GRACE?

The most important issue in resolving the problem of grace and its operation is to formulate the question properly, especially with regard to what is actually at stake. My contention is that it is not our individual sins as such that are the target of grace, but instead the state of sinfulness resulting from original sin, which precedes the commission of actual sin.[5] I have already argued that we are liable to punishment for all our

---

2. Or, at any rate, I hope to come as close as one possibly can to such an account within the limits of my insight. However, I stop short of a thorough discussion of grace in Catholic theology, restricting myself solely to the role of grace in counteracting the damage original sin has done to human nature. For more on the supernatural effects of grace, see, e.g., Hardon, *Theology of Grace*, 325–85, and Journet, *Meaning of Grace*, part 2.

3. Some Calvinists use the term "semi-Pelagian" to refer to any view that differs from their theological determinist position. As I use the term here, I am referring to the position condemned at the Council of Orange (529), according to which we can attract God's grace through doing our best to achieve sanctity on our own. I do not endorse this view and do not recognize any other sense to the term "semi-Pelagian." It is to be noted that some fair-minded Calvinists accept this; see Peterson and Williams, *Why I Am Not an Arminian*, 35–39.

4. See the figures mentioned in the preface to this book.

5. Actual sin does have a role to play in this matter subsequent to the receipt of grace according to the Catholic view, since actual sin can cause us to lose our salvation; however, I will take this up in the proper place; see below. In my opinion, the failure to distinguish between actual sin and original sinfulness has been a major source of confusion in the theology of grace. Christ's atoning death wins the forgiveness of all sins and earns infinite merit that can be applied to forgiven sinners by the Spirit in order to overcome their sinfulness (which still remains even after their actual sins are forgiven) and make silk purses out of sows' ears. See the text immediately following.

individual, freely chosen sins. In principle, God could forgive us those sins, and even remit the punishment for them in response to our sincere repentance and resolve to abjure those sins in the future, without effecting any change in our being.[6] Nevertheless, our original sinfulness remains, even if God does all of this, and it is this, rather than our actual sins *as such*, that cuts us off from our heavenly inheritance. It is this, then, that is the target of grace. The role of grace in salvation is to effect conversion and to cancel the effects of original sin by transforming our motivational structure, reorganizing it in such a way as to restore the right order of the parts of the soul and thus establishing love of God as the dominant motive for thought, feeling, and action in the human heart. Of course, the well-ordered soul will avoid actual sin as a matter of course, being no longer troubled by the disordered appetites, unruly passions, and inordinate desires that afflict and govern the sinful. Indeed, in the case of the blessed in heaven, who see and enjoy the presence of God, who is man's last end, sin will no longer even be possible. Grace, then, attacks sin at its root, which is sinfulness, rather than concerning itself with our actual past sins. In this respect, it is forward looking and concerned with our final salvation as such.

Despite the fact that we are not morally responsible for our original sinfulness itself and have no power within ourselves to counteract its overall influence, every human being is excluded thereby from the glory of God. In order to restore his image and likeness in us, God needs to intervene in the process; but merely forgiving us for our past actual sins will not solve the problem, since this will leave our disordered motivational structure unaffected and along with it our ineluctable tendency to sin. God's solution to this dilemma is the atoning death of Christ, which earns an infinite merit that the Father can apply for the redemption of sinners. This is God's freely given gift of grace, by means of which the Holy Spirit dwells within us.

Of course, God has no obligation to save any of us. In perfect justice, God could leave every human being in a fallen state without hope of recovery. Thankfully, the Christian God is the God of love and mercy who has not chosen to deal with his creatures in this way. His very act of creation is itself a free act of supererogation—something good to do but not morally required—and so an act of agapeistic love transcending

---

6. I say "in principle," but my actual opinion is that without the prior operation of God's grace, neither true contrition nor sincere amendment is a practical possibility.

(though not opposing) both reason and morality as such. In the same way, God deals with sinners, not by punishing them as he has every right to do, but instead by offering them his undeserved help that lies beyond their powers to earn. In the atoning death of Christ, God shows us in a most dramatic way *how much* he loves us and the extent to which he is willing to share our suffering by taking the punishment for our sins upon himself in order to thereby overcome the power of sin and death. In principle, of course, God need not have offered his saving help to everyone, but could have quite arbitrarily chosen on a more or less random basis to save some and not others, again without any strict injustice to anyone. However, given the testimony of God's love to the human race, it is not credible that the God worshiped by Christians would have done so. God wills that all human beings be saved and surely would make provision for this possibility, at least according to his antecedent will. We can only suppose that, if God gives his grace to anyone at all, he would give his grace to all without discrimination.

It does not follow that all men and women will be saved, however. Human beings retain their free will and thus have it within their power to reject God's unmerited gift of grace. Further, we have every good reason to suppose that some people have done so in the past and some will do so in the future. Some Christians reject this notion on the grounds that this is inconsistent with divine "sovereignty," preferring to adopt some sort of theological determinism. To do so, however, makes complete hash of the whole notion of sin and divine punishment. Indeed, if human beings did not have free will, then original *sin* would not have been possible in the first place, nor could we deserve eternal punishment for our actual sins, so without free will there would be no need for salvation. If we are caused to sin by forces outside of our control, even the decree of God's will, then we sin ineluctably and therefore do not deserve retributive punishment for having sinned.[7] Indeed, if anyone is responsible for that act, it can only be its agent cause. If God is cause of our sins through his

---

7. It is to be noted that compatibilists, no less than hard determinists, concede that their account of human "freedom" excludes the propriety of retributive punishment, guilt, and regret over the past and generally try to brazen it out by insisting that this is an advantage of their system, e.g., Dennett, *Elbow Room*, 153–72, and Smilansky, *Free Will and Illusion*, 222–27. For mainstream compatibilists, only therapeutic and/or deterrent punishments are legitimate. Since the eternal punishment of hell can only be retributive in character, it is doubtful whether any compatibilist account of the matter will be sufficient to justify the justice of that sort of punishment.

willing that we should commit them, then it is God, not we ourselves, who bears the ultimate moral responsibility for our sins. For God to punish us for what he has wrought through his own will would be the epitome of injustice. Despite the many attempts to evade or mitigate this conclusion, it remains the clear and evident implication of theological determinism in all of its forms, whether Protestant or Catholic.

If, as seems reasonable, one of God's ends in creating the universe was to make it possible for finite beings to know and love him, then God could not accomplish this without endowing those creatures with free will. Love cannot be commanded or compelled, or it is not genuine—only love freely given is truly expressive of the self. God gives his love to us freely, and all he asks is that we give our love to him freely in return, for our benefit rather than his own. For this reason, God gave us freedom. Due to the Fall and our current state of sinfulness, however, it lies beyond our power to use our freedom as God intended. Only if God gives us the means to do so will it be even so much as possible for us to give ourselves freely to God. This again is the work of grace, which does not cancel our freedom but enhances it in our weakened state in order to restore its full reality for us.

It is in this context God's decree of predestination must be understood. God's predestination cannot be the result of God being the efficient cause of our actions, whether directly or by means of irresistible grace. Instead, God's decree of predestination has to be the consequence of his infallible foreknowledge.[8] God undoubtedly foresaw the fall of

---

8. There is no room here to discuss the nature of divine foreknowledge, other than to say that I favor the view that God is timelessly eternal and knows all things by contemplating his own essence, which includes his free act of creation of a four-dimensional "block universe." On this view, there can be no literal *fore*knowledge or *pre*destination, because neither God nor the universe is in time, though I will continue to use this language throughout because time is a feature of our subjective conscious experience. The contingency of God's knowledge of contingent states of affairs is the consequence of his *scientia visionis*, which he possesses in virtue of the fact that God's act of creation terminates in the production of creatures. This knowledge is contingent because God need not have created this world, or have created at all. God, the ultimate *per se* cause of created beings, thus knows in accordance with his exhaustive knowledge of all possibilities, which of his conditional decrees (see below) are actualized by created free choice. In this way, God knows as eternally present what is future *to us* (from our subjective point of view) as its "physical" cause. This scientia visionis is nevertheless epistemically necessary for God, known by him with epistemic certainty from the eternal point of view in the same way as we perceptually know present events. Thus, God does not need to improvise, as open theists contend; neither does God need middle knowledge in

man, both as a pure possibility and as the actual consequence of the creation of the world. However, this does not mean that God is in any way at fault for having given us free will. For free will is a necessary condition for the possibility of our achieving the end for which God intended us. The Fall, by contrast, is merely the unintended but avoidable side-effect of that gift of freedom, the occurrence of which is neither the means to nor necessary for the achievement of that good end.[9] If we had not fallen, the divine plan would have proceeded without a hitch, conducting the entire human race to its last end. As it is, those who resist God's grace to the very end will be lost, though this was not necessary to the success of God's plan. Rather, those whom God infallibly foreknows to be lost will be lost through their own free choice, something that God merely permits to happen rather than positively decrees. To use the language of traditional theology, God *negatively* rather than positively reprobates those individuals, and if the sufferings of the damned glorify God by demonstrating his justice, that is God bringing good out of evil rather than bringing about evil so that good may come. God's antecedent will, in fact, would be better served if no one were damned. However, if God created us with free will, not even he can bring it about that no one is lost without overriding the free will of those who stubbornly refuse his offer of grace.

What, then, of those who are predestined to eternal life? God's antecedent will is that all human beings should accept his gift of grace, and to this end, he *conditionally* wills to save all human beings. However, God foresees that in the case of some human beings, the condition he stipulates (i.e., free and willing acceptance of God's gift of grace) will not be met and thus permits those souls to be lost through their own free choice, negatively reprobating those individuals. Those whom he infallibly foresees as freely accepting his gift of grace and thus meeting the condition he stipulates are thereby positively and categorically predestined to eternal life. Their sins are forgiven, and the punishment that they would otherwise deserve is remitted.[10] God's consequent will is

---

order to know our free choices in advance. He knows them as we make them.

9. As some of the "supralapsarians" contend, thus claiming that God deliberately wills evil so that good may come from it. Since it is always wrong to do evil so that good may come, to suppose this would be to question the absolute innocence of God.

10. To use traditional language, predestination is *ante praeviso meriti*, prior to foreseen merits; however, damnation is not *ante praeviso meriti*, but instead *post praeviso demeriti* due to one's resistance to grace; this is the view defended in Most, *Grace*. It

simply his antecedent, conditional will applied to and actualized in the case of individual human beings.

The usual objection to this picture is, once again, to claim that this is inconsistent with divine sovereignty, since it gives the created human will a decisive, even *the* decisive, role in determining whether he or she will be saved or damned. Of course, God remains sovereign even on this supposition. One should not think that God lacks the power to override the free will of his creatures. Indeed, it seems that God has occasionally done so in the past, though only for special reasons.[11] If God fails to do so in some particular case, then we must suppose that what happens as a result is in accordance with (that is, *permitted by*) the divine will even if not directly affected or approved by that will. God could have prevented it if he had so chosen. If he does not, then we must suppose that, for some good reason or other, God concurs with that choice. In the case of the individual who, actuated by grace and freed from sin, turns from it and embraces a life of faith and holiness, God positively approves of that individual's action as in accordance with his will and does not impede it. In the case of the stubborn soul that refuses God's help and decides to go it alone with inevitable disastrous consequences, God simply permits this to occur by not overriding the will of the sinner by *force majeur*. God, having willed to give us free will with full knowledge of the consequences, has also willed those consequences as he infallibly foresees them. As such, nothing that happens is contrary to God's will or beyond his power to alter through direct causal influence. Yet, if God has chosen through the exercise of his sovereign freedom, for our own good, that we should have free will and play some role in the attainment of our salvation, who are we to gainsay this? To do so would surely put limits on God's sovereignty understood as his ability to do whatever he chooses to do.

At the same time, let me hasten to add that this role must be carefully circumscribed and delineated in order to avoid granting too great a role to the created will. The account of free will outlined in the first part of this book does not treat free will as a positive, independent causal power capable of effecting changes in the world solely on its own initiative. As we saw, the employment of free will consists simply in our power to con-

---

does not follow from this that there is no need to atone for one's actual sins or pursue virtue as prompted by grace.

11. Exod 10:20.

trol or concentrate our attention by deliberately and voluntarily ceasing to attend to some of the contents of consciousness. This immanent act is simply a *ceasing* to do what we were doing before, an immanent act that indirectly produces a transeunt effect but not through the exercise of any efficient causal power. It thus does not need an efficient cause in order to account for its occurrence. In this way, then, we avoid the Banezian objection to free choice, which asserts that it involves impossibility insofar as it supposes that the creature exercises efficient causal power independently of God as First Cause.

Of course, the divine concurrence is required even for the possibility of the immanent act of free choice, since unless God concurs in our free decision to cease entertaining one or more of the alternatives, we will be unable to enact this choice. It is precisely in this way that God could overcome our free will. However, since God has given us free will precisely in order to make decisions of this sort possible for us, we may take it that God will only fail to concur with our free will when he has a special reason to do so. We may think of God's exhaustive knowledge of all possible states of affairs as containing all possible human actions and accompanied by conditional decrees (considered in the abstract) concerning whether or not God will concur with the production of that human action if someone freely chooses it. This will also extend to our sinful actions, insofar as they result from the exercise of free will. Once again, God's concurrence in the immanent act is indirectly productive of the sinful act as expressed in external behavior. It is not for the sake of producing the sin, but rather for the sake of the supreme good for which free will was given to us in the first place. The sin itself is only the foreseen but unintended consequence of that act of concurrence, thus permissible to God in accordance with the principle of licit double effect. The sin *as such* is mine and mine alone, inasmuch as I freely and knowingly chose it for the sake of enacting the external behavior expressive of my preference for the lesser over the greater good.[12] God is not, therefore, complicit in my sin, even though he permits it to occur when he might have prevented it and concurs in the production of the positive state of affairs that enacts that choice in reality. Neither is he morally responsible for it as he would be if he were its efficient cause.

We have clarified the question concerning grace. Now we need to turn to the relation between God's grace and free will in the case of the

---

12. Garrigou-LaGrange, *Predestination*, 324–35, actually explains this quite well.

justification of the elect, which is surely the most difficult problem in this area. Again, the goal is to establish God's grace as prior to and causally responsible for the production of saving faith in the elect without lapsing into theological determinism and altogether canceling the free cooperation of the will in effecting salvation. I shall contend that, while cooperation with God's grace does not involve a free action on the agent's part, but only the omission of an action that it was possible for that agent to perform, it is not something additional to the operation of grace itself. However, the rejection of God's grace does require an overt, if negative, act of will on our parts and is thus something that we do and thus for which we are responsible and can deserve punishment.

GRACE AND FREE WILL

It is only through the grace of Christ that it is possible for us to attain salvation. Yet as we have seen, we require salvation only if we have free will to begin with. There can be no question, then, of irresistible grace that simply negates our free will by overriding it, no matter how subtle and gradual its influence may be so that acceptance of that grace occurs with full compatibilist "freedom." If just damnation is possible only if we have the free will to *reject* God's offer of salvation, then so, too, will it be possible only if we can *freely* accept that offer. I really can see no way around this admission. Does this mean then that the human will is the decisive factor in determining our salvation? Perhaps it depends on what role free will plays in accommodating the operation of grace.

My contention is that our free will plays no direct role in aiding the operation of grace and that it is precisely in its mere acquiescence to the operation of grace that it cooperates with it.[13] In so doing, it does nothing overt or positive; nor indeed does it even act by *ceasing* to do anything. Its free acquiescence consists in nothing more than *its not doing something it might have done that lay within its power to do*, i.e., to resist the operation of grace.[14] Nevertheless, since it lay within its power

---

13. There is thus no "synergism" involved in the operation of grace, with the human will contributing some effort of its own and the rest being made up by God.

14. This is not the view of Scotus, according to which our cooperation with grace is free due to our continuing to possess the power to resist, though not the exercise of this power. (On this point, see Langston, *God's Willing Knowledge*, 36–38, and Cross, *Duns Scotus*, 150–51.) These two are inseparable in my view. If I cannot exercise a power, then I do not possess that power any more than I am rich if a perverse relative leaves me a million dollars in his will along with a codicil to the effect that I will forfeit the legacy if

to have performed this act even at the moment it omitted doing so, its cooperation, though not requiring overt behavior of any sort in addition to that produced by grace, is *free* in the full-blown sense of free to do otherwise.

However, the same is not the case where the rejection of God's grace is concerned. In that case, although it lay within my power to do otherwise by acquiescing in the operation of God's grace, I omit the salvific act, expressing and enacting my resistance to and rejection of God's grace by performing the *negative action* of turning away from the influence of grace. Since this is something that I *do*, albeit *negatively* by *ceasing to do* something I was previously engaged in doing, it represents a free and overt rejection of the offer of God's love in the form of his gift of salvation. Thus, my resistance is expressed in an act for which I am solely responsible and can be justly punished. Let us look into this in more detail.

In the first half of this book, I described how free will works as part of an overall account of the relation between mind and body. The exercise of free will is the consequence of the mental act of voluntary concentration of attention exercised with respect to our mental contents, taking the form of the negative action of *ceasing to entertain* one or more of the options for action available to me at a particular time. Consciousness consists of the activity of awareness, the content of which is produced through the activity of extramental processes occurring primarily in the brain. Among those spontaneously occurring mental contents are the various appetites, desires, and passions that motivate us to act in various ways. Some of these are instinctive or inherited tropisms or stereotypical behaviors, others are random, and still others we acquire through experience and practice. A small number of these are both novel and relevant to the situation, constituting sudden, brilliant inspiration as to what to do. In all such cases, however, the motive power is associated with an *action-pattern* already activated in the brain and requiring only our full attention in order to proceed into full-blown action. Concentration of attention, an immanent mental act that simply involves my ceasing to think about some of these spontaneously occurring contents, indirectly gives rise to a transeunt effect, not through being its efficient cause, but instead by eliminating one of the necessary conditions for an action-pattern to proceed into full-blown actualization in behavior. Concentration

---

I ever spend or invest a penny of it.

of attention is therefore a negative act, the causal consequence of an agent's deliberate and intentional "turning away" from some alternative by ceasing to entertain it. Even so, our turning away is still an act, i.e., something we do, even if we enact our "turning away" by a mere ceasing to do something that we were already doing.

Sometimes, however, there is no need to enact a free choice by doing anything, even a negative act. In many cases, for example, we simply acquiesce in following our strongest motive, by which I mean the motive we *feel* the strongest inasmuch as its intentional object is constituted as the most attractive among those currently available to my choice and experienced as at the center/forefront of conscious awareness. In such case, I simply allow myself to be led by my strongest motive, neither selecting it nor resisting it, but simply allowing it to carry me through its own phenomenological weight into full-blown enactment. In many cases, this happens automatically, without my even taking much notice of the fact. In other cases, it happens so quickly that I barely have time to register the fact; this will especially be the case when the behavior in question is instinctual or habitual. In other cases, however, it happens slowly, and I am fully conscious of the fact that I am being drawn to a certain overt action. While I could resist it, inasmuch as it lies within my power to turn away from that motive if I so choose, if I fail to do so, it will carry me along with it into enactment without my having to add anything to its operation.[15]

An example suggested by Henry Tappen, taken from ancient history, dramatically illustrates this point.[16] A king appoints his most faithful guard to watch over his beautiful but promiscuous wife. As soon as they are alone together, the woman begins to flirt with the guard and, over time, becomes increasingly bold in her advances on the loyal young

---

15. According to Lonergan, *Grace and Freedom*, 435–36, Aquinas contends that *gratia operans* is the irresistible cause of the act of will by means of which I produce the external act, for which the same grace serves as *gratia cooperans*. In this scheme of things, the human will is merely an instrument used by God to produce the external act and is "free" only in the compatibilist sense of voluntariness, as Lonergan himself admits. On the view presented here, Aquinas's account is correct with regard to the production of the external act. However, I place freedom of the will elsewhere than within the causal antecedents of the external act, simply as acquiescence in the operation of grace and nonresistance to its work, thus making the act genuinely free.

16. Tappan, *Doctrine of the Will*, 164–70. Tappan's case, taken from Herodotus, is much less dramatic than the one I have depicted here, which would make a good one-act opera.

man. Despite his best efforts, he finds his resolve weakening and realizes that he will not be able to resist her attractions for much longer. Finding himself caught in an irresolvable dilemma, pitting his loyalty to his king against strong sexual desire and finding his resolve to resist the King's wife weakening, the desperate young man takes his own life, thus drastically and forcefully preventing what would be the otherwise inevitable result. Of course, not every example of this is so extreme. In many cases, we see no reason why we should resist our strongest motive and not do as it prompts us. In others, reason approves our action and thus reinforces whatever nonrational motivation may be in play. Even in such cases, one's action remains a free one inasmuch as the power to resist remains intact.

In the case of a truly dominant motive, one's "window of resistance" may be limited, as in the above example. Unless one exercises one's option to resist by a certain point, there may be no turning back; beyond that point, one's power to resist a certain motive may no longer be sufficient to overcome that motive's momentum, which has now established full sway over oneself. At that point, what was formerly resistible may have become irresistible, so that its outcome is fully predictable by anyone properly placed to understand the forces in play. This does not prevent the action from being free or absolve the agent of responsibility for that act. Quite the contrary, just as it is the case that if one voluntarily took heroin for the first time, deciding to run the risk of future addiction, even though one is no longer free to resist the urge to take the drug on the hundredth occasion, one is nevertheless still at fault for doing so. In this way, then, an act that is irresistible for me on a certain occasion can still count as my free act because I failed to resist it during the time when it was still resistible, or failed to resist some preceding act that resulted in my doing this one. In such case, I am thus complicit in the fact that it is no longer resistible to me at the time I perform it and properly held morally responsible for it as well.

The foregoing helps us to better comprehend the mystery of God's grace without embracing theological determinism. Like the Banezians, we can admit that divine grace acts by physical premotion, setting our will into action prior to our consent. Like the Calvinists, we can admit that God's grace operates in such a way that it transforms our will so that, at the time that grace operates within us to produce justification, it is no longer resistible by the will and constitutes the sole and complete efficient cause of the saving act of faith. Nevertheless, this does not rule out the possibility that one's free will cooperates with grace through acquiescing to its influence, by not resisting it in circumstances in which it lay within one's power to do so. In so doing, it does nothing to alter or add to the operation of grace. As we noted earlier, the influence of the will in ordinary action in no way interferes with or contributes physically to the occurrence of the behavior that results from the forward progress of the action-pattern; the entire process is seamless on the horizontal level of efficient causality. The same is true of the operation of grace. From first to last, the operation of grace is the sole efficient cause of whatever it affects/effects. To use the language of the Schools, grace initially given is *sufficient* grace, i.e., grace sufficient for salvation if cooperated with/not resisted. With the passage of time, such grace becomes *efficacious* grace, at which point resistance is no longer possible. There is no reason to suppose that this may not happen at some point prior to the production of the salvific act itself. Even so, since that gracious physical premotion could have been resisted prior to that point and was not, the salvific act still counts as a free act. Since my only contribution to the occurrence of this act consists merely in the omission of an action I could have performed but did not, the entire positive reality of the salvific act, as well as its very occurrence, is the causal consequence of that premotion. It is thus more God's act than my own; my sole contribution to it lies simply in my acquiescence in letting it happen to me. The salvific action, then, is not something that I can boast in as though it were my own singular achievement.

As Maritain puts it, this physical premotion is a "shatterable" one, one that will carry through to enactment if left unopposed, but one to which I retain the capacity to prevent from doing so, at least at a certain stage.[17] If I decide either to turn away from the influence of grace for its own sake or to follow the lure of some other good, then I "shatter" that motion in so doing. By turning away from it and seeking the lesser good in preference to the greater one, I prevent that sufficient grace from becoming efficacious grace and retard its progress into enactment. Instead, whatever I have chosen in preference to that grace (which may simply be to decline its influence) gets the nod. On the other hand, if I simply do nothing and let the gracious physical premotion proceed through consciousness without turning away, then it will become irresistible at

---

17. Maritain, *Permission of Evil*, 1–43.

a certain point and achieve enactment through its own power by directly causing one's will to decree the salvific act. God's divine concurrence, then, is hardly a merely indifferent cooperation in this context. If I do nothing and thereby acquiesce in the operation of God's grace, then grace does everything for me.[18] On the other hand, if I turn away through the action of ceasing to entertain whatever it is that grace is prompting me to do—a *negative* action that, as we have seen, does not require an efficient cause—then God simply permits me to fall through my own free choice. This is something for which I am solely responsible and for which I alone must bear the consequences.

To put it another way, the role of the human will in the salvific context is merely *permissive*, rather than active. Human free will contributes to the production of saving faith only by allowing grace to do its work unhindered, providing merely a necessary condition for its operation. As such, it represents merely a background condition for the possibility of saving faith and is no more responsible for its production than the presence of oxygen is the (efficient or proximate) cause of a fire. Further, as I have just stated, by the time grace produces saving faith, free will may no longer be capable of resisting its operation and so is powerless to impede the operation of grace in the soul.

Grace operates to produce faith by persuading us internally of the truth of the Gospel and its message. This initial *conversion* from unbeliever to believer may have an intellectual component (such as the traditional *praeambula fidei* that for some people are a source of grace). However, it is essentially a matter of grace turning us away from the selfishness, pride, and hard-heartedness constituting our primary defenses against the love of God in order that we might experience and enjoy that love. Thus, God liberates us from sin in order that we may freely love him. Unlike the false "autonomy" that attempts to put the self, its fallible reason, and distorted motivational structure at the center of reality, grace liberates us to abandon ourselves in obedience to God, an act that, far from taking away our liberty, is in fact true empowerment.

The response of the will to grace is not to choose to believe the Gospel with its help; instead, it is, as a result of the preparation of grace, to be able truly to say, "Not my will, Lord, but yours be done." Grace operates by *attracting* us, whether by degrees or (in rare cases) all at once,

---

18. This does not imply that I am merely passive in relation to grace, since grace prompts me to strenuous action; see Chapter 6 below.

to the Gospel and its teachings, an attraction that at some point becomes our dominant motivation, then finally overcomes all other contrary motives altogether. At this point, we desire to believe more than anything that might have been preferred to it. In the face of the lure of this now irresistible grace, the will abandons its pretensions to self-control and, instead of choosing for itself, abandons itself, submits to the will of God, and allows itself to be led by grace into faith, handing itself over to the Spirit. Thus, as St. Paul says, "It is no longer I who live, but it is Christ who lives in me, and the life I live in the flesh I live by faith in the Son of God."[19] Still, human free will has played its part in bringing this happy state of affairs about simply by not impeding the process of initial conversion when it might have, at a time when groundless fear and the lure of sin tempted us to do so. Thus, saving faith is not the product of free choice, though human free will does play a role in making it possible. At the same time, faith is a gift from God, the product of the operation of grace in the human soul. To believe, then, is not an *intrinsically* meritorious act on our part, though, as in the case of Abraham, it is credited to us as righteousness for our Lord's sake, in accordance with his salvific will for each of us and the promises that he has made to those who believe in him.[20]

Just as God can permit evil without being morally culpable for so doing, so too does the human will, in cooperating with God's grace, contribute to personal salvation without acquiring merit through its own efforts for any act prompted by grace, including the initial salvific act of faith. In a similar manner, human nonresistance, which requires no action on our part (not even a negative one of turning away from other motivations, since grace accomplishes even this for us), serves merely as the necessary condition for the production of saving faith. As such, we do nothing for which we can claim any merit on our own behalf independently of the working of grace for *any* positive act we do, such as believing the Gospel. My free cooperation with grace amounts to no more than my not rejecting it by exercising my free choice in such a way as to turn away from the influence of grace, thus choosing the lesser over the greater good. Therefore, I cannot claim any merit for myself on that

---

19. Gal 2:20 (NAB).

20. This is the *condign* and *congruous* merit attaching to good works in Catholic theology; see, e.g., Hardon, *Theology of Grace*, 297–301.

score alone, even though I am partly responsible for the fact that I am, at some point, justified by faith.

After all, I don't deserve any credit or reward *simply* for refraining from doing wrong, such as robbing banks or committing adultery. I have even less claim to moral merit if my not robbing banks or committing adultery requires a great moral effort on my part. If I have any conscience at all, from the very fact that I am strongly attracted to the idea of robbing banks or committing adultery, I ought already to be condemned in my own eyes as morally deficient, weak, and vicious. That I am able to muster enough "willpower" to resist these desires is certainly better than giving in to them, but I hardly deserve moral credit or some sort of reward for doing so. I deserve it even less if my *motive* for so doing was something like fear of being caught, loss of reputation, or self-interested calculation.

In this vein, we note that the same applies to the standard dismissal of Pascal's wager as a crass appeal to fear of divine punishment and self-interested desire for an infinite reward as the motive for religious belief. This is the consequence of a failure to understand the rhetorical strategy of Pascal's wager. Once we understand this strategy, we can see that this objection is completely unfair to Pascal. Pascal addresses his wager to his libertine gambler friends, all of whom are sinners and for whom only self-interested motives for action can make any appeal. Pascal is trying to convince them that, even from their own distorted point of view, it still makes good sense not to embrace religious belief as such (Pascal, as an Augustinian Christian, believes that faith is the gift of God through grace), but instead to consider *seriously* the claims of the Gospel. It is for this that Pascal intends the rest of the *Pensées* to provide the positive evidence. Of course, the operation of grace will eventually replace fear and hope of reward with genuine love of God as the motive for faith in God—fear of the Lord is the *beginning* of wisdom, not its sum and substance. Further, despite his Jansenism, Pascal was Catholic enough to believe that it is through the Sacraments and the Sacramentals ("masses and holy water") that God has primarily ordained to dispense those graces. Thus, Pascal is not cynically recommending fear of punishment and hope of gain as legitimate motives for belief. Quite the contrary, it is precisely because his intended audience has no capacity to respond to any other suasion that forces him to make this sort of appeal. It is not Pascal or his appeal that is at fault, but instead those whom he hopes to evangelize and convert. Yet Pascal's critics inevitably want to project these motives on Pascal himself, who actually showed no trace of them in his own spiritual life.

Most of us are likely to think ourselves better than the "tough customers" who were the object of Pascal's evangelization—although I suspect many of us are self-deceived about this. However, if one is, like Pascal, an Augustinian Christian, then one realizes that prior to the operation of grace, there is no natural capacity for sincere love of God, our neighbors, and ourselves for his sake, the only motive for belief that is truly acceptable to him. As such, the soul of the yet-to-be regenerated sinner possesses no merit-conferring motives for belief through which his or her free acquiescence to the operation of grace in the soul can be produced. Indeed, such a soul possesses only morally disreputable motives, such as fear of punishment or long-term self-interest, which can possibly counterbalance the pressing demands of the immediate promptings of our sin-disordered motivational structure. Thus, the only motives available to us by nature to support us in our acquiescence to the operation of God's grace are morally disreputable ones incapable of conferring moral worth on that action.[21] Thus, to the extent that our cooperation with grace is the product of our own efforts rather than the attraction of grace itself, that cooperation is salutary in its effect but not a source of moral merit. That is because the act is not done from the right motive, which motive itself is not possible for us prior to regeneration and is itself the product of the influence of God's habitual grace. That some of our nonmoral motives are available to aid us in acquiescing to the influence of God's grace is fortunate and another case in which God brings good out of evil. In this context, God acts in the same manner as Hegel's cunning of reason, which according to some Hegel scholars uses violence and irrationality to undermine themselves and achieve the ends of reason. Nevertheless, this again is God's doing and not our own, so not something for which we can claim—or deserve—credit. The point is this: To the extent that I contribute anything of my own to the motivation that inspires my nonresistance, those motives (such as fear or hope of reward) are morally disreputable and thus no ground for merit. To the extent that my choice is informed by meritorious motives, such as love of God for his own sake, the presence of that motivation is due to pre-

---

21. These are still "graces" of a sort, i.e., gifts of God in our fallen state, but not the product of supernatural grace.

venient grace and thus not something for which I am responsible or can claim any moral credit. It is thus not a meritorious work on my part.

Something similar obtains in the case of those who are lost. It is sufficient for me to resist God's grace that I simply *not act* as grace prompts me to do in those circumstances in which it lay within my power to have acquiesced to its influence. This again is merely an omission, a failure to do something that lay within one's power to do. Through grace, God has given the creature the power to perform the salvific act, not through its own causality but through the cooperation with grace that I have just been describing.[22] The essence of the creature's rejection of God consists simply in not performing that act in circumstances in which it lay within that creature's power to do so, operating as a secondary cause in the service of the divine will. This is something I can bring about without concentrating my attention on any other positive act, but simply through ceasing to entertain the salvific act itself. This negative act of concentration of attention is merely the *means* through which I shatter the premotion of sufficient grace and thus prevent what would otherwise become its efficacious effect. It expresses and enacts, rather than constitutes, my free decision not to do as grace prompts, which while being merely the omission of the salvific act, is nevertheless the choice of the lesser over the greater good.[23]

Undoubtedly, the choice to omit the salvific act flows from a defect of the will that prompts us not to cooperate with sufficient grace as its principle. However, since the will is free, this provides only a causally necessary, not a causally sufficient, condition for that choice. Through the power of grace enabling free choice, we could have resisted the temptation represented by that defect of will in those circumstances. Failure to do so is neither God's fault—he has done everything that love can do in these circumstances—nor the result of some irresistible defect of will for which God is ultimately responsible. In the case of those who are lost, then, sinners freely choose the lesser good in preference to the greater good in circumstances in which it lay within their power to have

---

22. Pontifex, *Freedom and Providence*, 68–69.

23. This negative act still requires the divine concurrence, consisting in God's not preventing my concentration of attention, brought about by my ceasing to entertain the salvific act, thus "hardening my heart" in such a way as to make that concentration of attention possible. God's permissive concurrence is a necessary condition for my heart being hardened, hence cannot occur without it; in this way, God hardens whom he will harden without it being the case that his hardening *causes* the sinner to reject God.

done otherwise. As such, they are causally responsible for their dereliction and thus bear the entire moral responsibility for so doing.[24]

Since I enact my decision to reject God's grace simply by ceasing to entertain the positive actions, both interior and exterior, to which grace prompts me, the act by means of which I reject God's grace is a merely negative act that does not need an efficient cause. Further, since it does not consist in the exercise of a positive causal power, it does not require a concurrence that sustains that power in the period between the exercise of that power and its application to the effect. Rather, the divine concurrence here is merely permissive. It consists solely in God's not overriding my free will by continuing to sustain my attention to the rejected alternative contrary to my decision to do otherwise. Again, God could do this and may sometimes do so, but only in extraordinary circumstances. Freedom of the will is thus preserved, and the sinner bears the sole responsibility for his or her damnation. Since free will is a necessary condition for the possibility of a genuinely loving response to God, he grants his concurrence, permitting sin as the unintended by-product of its misuse, a misuse that God cannot systematically prevent through overriding our free will without undermining the very good for which he gave us free will in the first place.

In this way, we secure the absolute innocence of God in the production of sin.[25] Along with it, we make the eternal punishments of hell, understood precisely as retributive punishment, intelligible in the case of those who freely reject God's offer of salvation with full knowledge and consent of the will. Such people have chosen to remain in their sinfulness and, through their freely chosen and unrepented sins, earned eternal separation from God, embracing the misery of their condition in preference to his love. Although the saved will recognize the absolute justice of the plight of the damned, there will be no joy in heaven over their suffering.

I think I have said enough to dispel the notion that our free cooperation with God's grace is intrinsically meritorious and to distinguish our act of cooperation with God's grace from our act of resistance to it. The first is no act, positive or negative, but merely the omission of an

---

24. Thus, *contra* Hartley, it is not the case that, if one is blameworthy for rejecting God's grace, one's acceptance of that grace is therefore intrinsically meritorious; see Hartley, *Observations on Man*, part 2, 56–66.

25. Maritain, *Permission of Evil*, 3–11.

act that it lay within our power to perform. The second, though a negative act undertaken to secure the omission of another act in accordance with a prior decision, is still an immanent mental act that gives rise to a transeunt effect leading to reprobation, or damnation. Whatever is meritorious in either our motives or our actions is the product of grace reflecting the all-sufficient merit of Christ our redeemer; whatever we contribute confers no moral worth on our actions, however saving they may be. Still, for most Christians, this is not the end of the story. Growth in the Christian life is an ongoing conversion, a process of progressive *sanctification* in which we are transformed from sinners into saints. It is to that part of the process we now turn.

6

Sanctification

FAITH, WORKS, AND THE NATURE OF MERIT

A MAN FALLS OFF an ocean liner into the freezing ocean. The cold water quickly saps his strength, and he begins to drown. Suddenly, a life ring, towline attached, appears out of the fog, landing in the water next to him. "Grab ahold!" he hears a voice call out, "I will pull you to safety." Although he is going under, the man makes a desperate lunge and manages to grab hold of the life ring. Immediately the towline goes taut, and some unseen hand begins to pull him toward safety. The man is extremely tired and weak; it requires all of his concentration simply to stay awake. However, whenever he is about to drift off, let go of the life ring, and sink beneath the waves, he hears the voice of his unseen rescuer saying, "Hold on! Don't give up! Just a little longer and I promise you will be all right." Although he loosens his grip and even lets go of the life ring on a couple of occasions, the encouragement of the rescuer keeps him from giving up; he grasps the life ring again and is eventually pulled to safety.

Keep this story in mind as you read what follows. It is a metaphor for the operation of grace in the process of salvation. We will return to it at the end of this chapter.

FAITH AND SAVING FAITH

Faith, understood as saving belief, is the first fruit of the operation of grace in the souls of the elect. Obviously, no one can possibly achieve salvation without some inkling of the saving truth: *orthodoxy* precedes *orthopraxy*. Still, we must not place *a priori* limits on the power or extent of God's grace and its operation. There is implicit as well as explicit faith, more or less perfectly grasped by non-Christians and testified to by the overlap in ethical teaching among the world's great religions, which is itself testimony to the universality of conscience as the voice of God in every human breast.[1] Further, there is clear testimony that there are non-Christians who live morally good lives and perform right actions from motives that any Christian would have to approve. Although some Christians insist that only those who have made a conscious commitment to Christ as their savior and have received the Gospel as saving truth can be saved, the wiser part seems to recognize that the mystery of salvation exceeds our understanding. If God antecedently desires to save all human beings, we must assume that he gives the grace of Christ, in some form or other, to all human beings regardless of their cultural or religious background. However, at the same time, we must affirm that whoever is saved is so through the grace of Christ, regardless of whether he or she apprehends this fact.[2] Nevertheless, in what follows I will concern myself solely with salvation as it occurs within an exclusively Christian context.

Although conversion is sometimes associated primarily (and, for some Protestants, exclusively) with the initial act by means of which faith, in the sense of an occurrent belief in the truth of the Gospel message acquired through the operation of grace, the fact seems to be that conversion is an ongoing process. To be saved surely requires more than a one-time altar call or signing and dating the profession of faith contained in the back of a free copy of the Gideon Bible. Even among some evangelicals, we find the recognition that faith, understood as *saving faith*, includes more than mere belief or even subjective certainty that one is "saved." Saving faith is not just belief, but as the *Epistle of James* puts it, a faith that naturally and ineluctably expresses itself in works, in particular, the works that grace prompts us to perform as part of the ongoing process of *sanctification*, by means of which we are progressively transformed by grace from sinners into saints.[3] Conversion, then, refers more properly to this entire process, of which the sort of conversion

---

1. C. S. Lewis, *Miracles*, Appendix, 93–121.

2. See Griffiths, *Problems of Religious Diversity*, 56–64, 159–61, on this point.

3. Jas 2:14–26. Verse 24 explicitly states that we are *not* justified by faith apart from works. What is needed is not further wrangling about "faith alone" and "works righteousness" but clarifying the relation between these equally necessary elements in the mystery of salvation.

known as justification *through* faith (where faith is restricted simply to the mental act of belief, i.e., occurrent assent to the truth of the Gospel message as such, even with deep inwardness and complete subjective certainty) is only the initial stage. It is only in the full-blown sense in which saving faith includes the works prompted by grace and expressive of our assent to the Gospel that we are saved by faith. Only at the end of this process are we truly said to be saved *by* the grace of Christ.

We can see, then, that when properly understood, there can be no real opposition between faith on the one hand and works on the other. Both are the products of grace, rather than unaided human effort, and our contribution to their occurrence is no more than our merely allowing grace to operate by not opposing it. The influence of the Holy Spirit prompts our good works and accomplishes them through us by means of grace. We need do no more than permit grace to work the Father's will in us, and it will be accomplished through the power of Christ's merit by the workings of the Holy Spirit. This process, then, needs no additional contribution from us in order to carry us to the fullness of salvation. It does not follow from this, of course, that we need fall into the error of quietism, supposing that the height of piety is realized in apathetic inactivity. The great exertions of the saints, prompted by the inspiration of grace and informed throughout by its energy, attest to the fact that the life of grace, while a response to divine prompting, is nevertheless also a life of intense activity as well.

At the same time, since it is grace rather than our own effort that produces these works, the moral credit for them belongs to God rather than to us. God works *through* us to accomplish his will and to realize his plan for the human race; we are merely the means, or instrument, for his will rather than agents acting in our own right. Just as the credit for a good deed done by a servant at his master's behest goes to the master (as primary agent) rather than to the servant (who is merely a means, or instrument), so too does the credit for the good works that we do through the power of grace redound to the economic Trinity that accomplishes those works by means of the faithful. After all, obedience to the will of God is our natural duty, and no one deserves praise or credit *merely* for doing one's duty, however much one may be liable to punishment for failing to do so. If we can claim any moral merit for our good works, this can only be because they are done from the right motive, namely, love of God and of neighbor. However, given that love of God is itself the product of grace, it belongs to us only as a gift of God and not as something that we can claim on our own account. Our good works *as such*, then, are less ours than they are God's and more to his credit than ours, so that no one has cause to boast about the good works that one does through the power of Christ's grace. Rather, like the great saints, we need to realize that the more good we do through the influence of the Holy Spirit, the greater should be our appreciation of God and the more humble we ought to be about ourselves. Even at our best, we are unworthy servants, not because we fail to do what God calls upon us to do, but only because our ability to carry out his will is so limited.[4]

However, this raises a problem. God clearly wants us to do good works, even promising to reward us in accordance with them at the Last Judgment.[5] Works, therefore, cannot be regarded as altogether irrelevant to the process of salvation. Yet if we do not earn salvation through good works, laying up "treasures in heaven" by doing what we are told to do in such a way as to earn moral credit for our actions in hope of getting a reward when we die, what possible role could works play in the salvific scheme? It is to this question that we shall now turn.

THE ROLE OF WORKS IN SALVATION

St. Paul constantly tells us that we are justified by faith, not works. We do not *earn* our salvation by doing good works through our own power. At the same time, it hardly seems credible that it is sufficient for salvation simply to believe with our minds that Christ died for our sins. This view would be consistent with a thoroughgoing antinomianism, according to which nothing at all would be required in order for us to be saved, a view that not even Luther was willing to embrace. Even if we join this idea to the notion that God calls us to do certain things out of love for him, unless these actions are somehow directed to our benefit, there would seem to be completely arbitrary demands that are thoroughly dispensable for us, since nothing affecting our salvation flows from their omission. Even if we further qualify this by claiming that God's grace naturally leads us

---

4. It does not follow, of course, that we are morally culpable for this; regret at not being able to do more is not guilt. Not even God requires us to do more than we can possibly do, regardless of how much we would like to be able to do. We can only be obliged to do what it is that, with God's prompting and help, lies within our power to do.

5. Matt 25:31–46. Any work of standard Catholic apologetics will contain the rest of the Catholic "proof texts" on this issue.

to do these actions as expressive of our faith in him, unless there is some reason for God's grace to prompt these actions in us, there seems little if any reason for God to do so. The complete disconnect between works and salvation, then, hardly seems credible.

I believe I can explain how works can contribute to salvation without being either the result of individual effort apart from the influence of grace or in such a way as to provide intrinsic moral merit for the agent who performs them through the power of grace working in them. Works do contribute to salvation, not with respect to justification as such, but rather in the context of sanctification. Due to original sin, we come into the world with an already disordered motivational structure that reflects a self-centered rather than God-centered perspective on reality, one that expresses itself in our inner thoughts, our words, and our external actions, no matter how much we attempt to disguise our true selves from others and even from ourselves. Because of our sinfulness, every human being over the age of reason is an actual sinner. These actual sins further corrupt our motivational structure, driving us further from God, and this dynamic, if left unchecked, will inevitably lead to irreversible damage to our souls.[6] At that point, we will be irrevocably lost, beyond the power even of God's grace to recover. Beyond justification, the forgiveness of our sins by God that restores the right relation between God and creature, there is the task of repairing the damage done by sin and overcoming our original sinfulness. This is the main task, because the ingression of sinfulness into the human motivational structure is so extensive that even those who are justified are incapable of any significant participation in the life of God, let alone the heavenly banquet to which God calls us. Beyond the forgiveness of our sins achieved by Christ's atoning death and the justification wrought by grace through faith, we need rehabilitation as well in order to be fit for heaven, where nothing that is not holy may enter.

Just as our souls were first corrupted by works—freely chosen acts of dereliction—so too it must be by works that our souls are realigned and restored to health. Good works are the means by which the process of sanctification is accomplished in us, through the reorientation of our motivational structure from that which we inherit because of original sin and further damage through actual sin to that which makes us fit for our heavenly inheritance. What makes those works to be good *in this context*

---

6. See Pieper, *Concept of Sin*, and references.

is not that they are in accordance with the natural moral law, although it is precisely because they are good in this sense that they are capable of accomplishing our sanctification. Rather, these count as good works in this context because they are the kinds of acts capable of reestablishing the reign of reason in our souls. It is precisely for this reason that God commands them. Just as sin disorders and stains the soul with its evil, so too do good works counteract the effect of sin, remove that stain, and make it possible for us to love God as reason tells us that we ought.

At the same time, good works are the product of grace rather than unaided free will. It is only because God's grace premoves the will that we can even conceive of doing those good works, let alone find it within our power actually to accomplish them. Indeed, as I have already argued, it is really the Holy Spirit, through the grace of Christ, who is performing those works by means of my will. Though they are done voluntarily, with full consent of the will (itself the product of the operation of grace in which one has freely acquiesced), they can be called one's own acts only by a kind of courtesy, since the human agent performing them is neither their first efficient cause nor contributes materially in any way to their production. In this context, the human agent is like a pen wielded by the President when he signs a treaty; it acts merely as an instrumental, secondary cause in relation to God, who prompts that act through grace. However, for these acts to effect sanctification does not require anything more than this. Since these acts are done by, in, and through one's own will, they are able to produce a residual effect in the soul of the agent who performs them, which by degrees reorganizes and reorients its motivational structure in such a way as to engender genuine virtue and love of God. Grace operates in such a way as to replace one's obdurate heart of stone with a heart of flesh, one that knowingly and willingly obeys God and longs in confident hope for its last end, the beatific vision. One cooperates freely with the operation of grace in this context only by not opposing it through omitting any act of resistance to that operation. In so doing, the will expresses its freedom through acquiescence, rather than through a negative act of selection, allowing grace to do with it as it will.

Sanctification does not normally happen in a moment. Rather, it is the consequence of the acquisition of the moral and the infused theological virtues. These habits of thought and action make their appearance in the forms of spontaneous judgments and feelings and naturally express themselves in external behavior. These virtuous traits alter our appetites and desires by changing the manner and aspect in which their objects appear to us, thus realigning our motivational structure in such a way that it conforms to the dictates of reason and the will of God. This is accomplished through repeated action, because of which the performance of the right action from the right motive becomes easy, pleasant, and at last the true expression of one's inner self. These virtues include, but are not limited to, the classical moral virtues—prudence, temperance, courage, and justice. They also include the theological virtues (faith, hope, and charity) and related virtues, such as humility, piety, modesty, and religion, all of which Hume despised. To acquire these virtues is to become a saint and to be prepared for the glories of heaven in which sinners can take no pleasure. At this point, only compatibilist "freedom" remains, and sin is no longer even possible for the saved.

Grace produces this effect as a by-product of its main operation, which is to premove the will to perform good works in accordance with God's will for the furtherance of his plan for salvation. These include moral actions but also extend to the specifically religious actions of prayer, praise, sacrifice, and participation in the sacraments, especially the communal celebration of the liturgy. However, not even these latter are arbitrarily willed for their own sakes, or for God's. God, after all, has no need of our prayers or worship; being perfect, God already lives in unapproachable glory and infinite happiness that lies not within our power to augment or decrease. Nor does God lack anything that requires our service or praise. Finally, neither would God require us to perform good works, praise, and worship him for no reason at all or merely to boss us around like some whimsical tyrant. Rather, whatever God wills us to do is directly for *our* sakes, not for his. God desires that we should perform good works, pray, and worship him because, in so doing, we become more God-like and thus by degrees more closely approximate our natural end and approach the perfection necessary to be worthy of our supernatural one, the possession and enjoyment of eternal life with God. The more we reflect the divine nature, the more God sees himself in us and the more he rejoices in that fact out of selfless love for us.[7] At the same time, we further glorify God through the attainment of the perfection of our nature, which participates in God's own nature, in

---

7. Thus, it is the case that God loves his elect more than he does sinners, since they realize the image and likeness of God in themselves to a higher degree. However, this differential love is not the *cause* of election, but rather its consequent.

whose image and likeness we were made.[8] God wills us to do those acts of duty and piety that are sufficient to sanctify us in order that we might receive the heavenly kingdom that he has prepared for us as a reward for accomplishing his ends in the world. Of course, God could achieve these external ends much more directly and effectively simply through his own *fiat*; however, God has chosen to use us as the means to achieve those ends so that we might both glorify him and be made worthy of heaven.

Kant argues that we cannot interpret the Golden Rule as the duty to love others as we love ourselves because love *as an inclination* cannot be commanded; how we feel, he contends, is not under the control of our wills.[9] I think Kant is wrong about this. God can command us *really* to love one another because he stands ready to give us, through grace, the means to accomplish this end. Although we cannot love others simply by willing to do so, by doing grace-prompted works of charity and good for others, we can by degrees become people who do, in fact, love our neighbor out of an inclination that is the by-product of our life in grace. A life of obedience to God, then, is also a life in pursuit of virtue (the by-product of that obedience) and happiness (the greatest fulfillment and felicity it is possible for us to achieve), supervening (as Aristotle says) "like the bloom of youth on those in the flower of their age."[10] Grace initiates the process, at first conforming the will to the rigors of obedience; as time goes on, however, the attitude of obedience is by degrees replaced with the internalized ideal of loving service to others out of love of God—the theological virtue of charity characteristic of the lives of the great saints. For such persons, to do the will of God is neither difficult nor onerous but truly second nature, approximating the perfection of our original nature. For the sanctified, the yoke is easy and the burden light. Only such souls are truly prepared for, and capable of enjoying, heavenly life with God.

MERIT

The question of merit is another perplexing issue that arises in discussions of the operation of grace. On the one hand, if virtue is the consequence of the operation of grace, itself the free gift of God, then we can claim nothing for ourselves on its behalf, because human effort plays

---

8. See Edwards's account of this in Faust and Johnson, *Edwards Selections*, 340-71.

9. Kant, *Grundlegung* 399, 15–22. Of course, Kant was not uniformly wrong; there is much of value in his moral philosophy.

10. See chapter 4, note 11.

little if any direct role in its acquisition. We can hardly claim to have *earned* heaven as the just recompense for our good works, which would essentially tie God's hands in such a way that he would be morally obliged to give it to us on that account. At the same time, the Scriptures assure us that God demands good works from us, gives us the means through which we can perform those works, and will reward us in accordance with those works. The Scriptures clearly teach that those without good works cannot enter the Kingdom of God and are excluded from heaven for their unrepented sins. As such, the performance of good works appears to be both necessary for salvation and sufficient to qualify us for a posthumous reward in heaven. It is difficult to avoid the implication that merit attaches to our good works in some fashion. Yet, if merit in this context is not the merit of personal desert earned through our own individual efforts apart from God's grace, then what sense is to be made of that notion in this context?

The answer lies in the realization that not all merit is a consequence of effort and not all deserts are Kantian moral deserts. One can sometimes deserve something simply on the grounds that one possesses certain features or characteristics, even though one has done nothing (or at any rate very little) to earn them. The following example will illustrate this point.

Suppose that a small town in the mountains needs a doctor but is unable to attract an outsider to take the post. In their extremity, the citizens of that town decide to choose one of their own and have him or her trained as a doctor on the promise that the individual chosen returns to the town to practice. The choice comes down to two candidates. One candidate is imbued with a spirit of public service, good at physics and chemistry, sensitive, intelligent, and hard working, and on top of that, he *really wants* to be a doctor. The other is a good fellow, would probably make an adequate medical practitioner, and just happens to be the mayor's son but is nowhere near as talented or dedicated as his rival for the position is. Intuitively, it seems unjust to overlook the well-qualified candidate in favor of the mayor's son. More than this, it seems it would be *positively wrong* to deny the more-qualified candidate the position—he clearly deserves it and thus has a legitimate claim to it that ought to be honored.

One might suppose that this intuition must be grounded in some sort of moral desert residing in the superior candidate. This need not be so, however. Perhaps his intellectual abilities are the result of his native endowments and are thus merely gifts of fortune. Perhaps his attractive personal traits, capacity for hard work, and desire to be a doctor are the consequence of his early childhood training and the presence of good role models who encouraged him to develop these attitudes and characteristics, something that he would never have done without these fortunate circumstances. However, even if we suppose that his own contribution to his possession of these traits and characteristics is utterly negligible, it still does not change the fact that they are the relevant grounds for the assignment of this position, along with all the benefits and burdens that it entails. It is something he therefore deserves simply through his possession of the relevant characteristics, regardless of whether or not he can claim any *personal merit* for his possessing them. Thus, one can have a legitimate claim to something and thus deserve it as a matter of justice, despite the fact that one has done nothing whatsoever to earn it through one's own efforts due to its being the product of morally arbitrary factors. We might call this sort of merit the "merit of appropriateness" (one sense of the term "condign merit") as opposed to moral merit. It is appropriate that God should reward those who possess the virtues with the gift of eternal life, because they are the ones who, through the possession of the sanctity and holiness produced by those virtues, are suited for the life of heaven and prepared to both enjoy and participate in its glories. Those who lack those characteristics have no claim on it, nor is it appropriate that it should be given to them. As such, they are rightly excluded from eternal life with God for that reason alone. That is why original sin is sufficient to cut us off from God and eternal life and why the atoning death of Christ (or something equivalent) was necessary in order to open the gates of heaven to the human race.

It does not follow from this that eternal punishment in hell can be justified on the same basis, so that the damnation of sinners is itself simply another application of the merit of appropriateness. Retributive punishment, the only sort of punishment that the irrevocable and eternal punishments of hell could possibly be, by its very nature requires personal responsibility for one's actions, something lacking in those caught in the grips of forces outside of their control by means of which they were unable to avoid sinning. Even if all of our sins are freely chosen, since the Fall we do not have a choice about whether or not we will sin, even if every sin we commit was avoidable in principle. Since the children of

Adam and Eve are not personally morally responsible for original sin, one does not deserve eternal punishment on that score, even if the vision of God in paradise could be denied on that basis. Further, given the fact of human sinfulness, even if we sin freely and we are culpable for our individual sins as such, this does not justify eternal punishment in itself, since none of our sins can merit eternal punishment considered in themselves. Eternal separation from God can only be the result of an irrevocable free choice to remain in one's sinfulness by rejecting God's free offer of help to overcome sinfulness through acquiescence in his grace. Only in this way can our sinfulness be both permanent and irrevocable for us while at the same time be something for which we are culpable. Only sinfulness of this sort can merit eternal damnation. It does not follow from this that salvation must also be a matter of moral desert. The same holds *vice versa* as well; just because salvation is not a matter of moral merit, it does not follow that reprobation cannot be such.

Although God is not obligated to save anyone, a loving God, in whose image we were made, would obviously want to save all and extend his help to all out of love for us. It is fully reasonable, then, to think that God offers his grace to all human beings in accordance with his antecedent will, regardless of their condition or circumstances. Even so, given that we have free will, it thus lies within our power to reject God's offer of salvation and thus earn our reprobation through the misuse of that free will. Only in such case, then, will reprobation be a matter of moral desert and the unending punishment of the damned justified.

Merit, then, is a consequence of sanctification, a further by-product of the process by means of which we are conformed to the image of God within us, which is itself the full expression of our human nature both with regard to its natural and its supernatural ends. This merit gives the sanctified a just claim to the reward of eternal life, without the need for any personal desert on their part, other than that which is the product of the operation of grace, itself a free gift from God. However, this does not mean that God is bound to give them heaven or morally obligated to give them this reward regardless of his will. For God sent his Son to die for our sins precisely so that he could give us this boon out of love for us. God's only obligation is to himself that no one who is not worthy should stand in his heavenly presence. The merit of the saved is not the cause of their receiving the reward of heaven, but instead merely the necessary condition for its being conferred upon them, a necessary condition that has been established in them by grace, itself the supererogatory gift of God, earned not through their acts, but instead through the moral merit of Christ's redeeming death. God, out of supererogatory love, has done for us what we could not do for ourselves. Since the merit attending our acts is caused, not insofar as the acts are ours, but instead as they are the consequences of the operation of grace in us, we have no ground either to boast of our virtue or to demand a reward from God. We may nevertheless feel perfectly confident that God, who wants to confer heaven on us so passionately that he died for our sins, will confer that reward on all those who freely cooperate with his sanctifying grace. It is for this reason that God has promised these rewards to those who love him and obey his will.

PERSEVERANCE

What I have been suggesting so far is that the operation of grace is completely smooth and untroubled—that once we make the initial act of faith, God's grace simply takes over, and there is neither necessity for any further struggle nor any possible threat to our salvation after that point. This, of course, is not what we actually experience. No matter how powerful our initial conversion experience may be, it nevertheless remains that growth in the Christian life is beset with struggle, setbacks, and continual failure. Along with this, there are healthy doses of guilt, self-recrimination, and an ongoing need for forgiveness on the part of God for our subsequent transgressions as well as to perform penance for our misdeeds. The Old Man dies hard even as grace struggles to bring the New Man to birth within us. To judge by appearances, at least, there are those who make a hopeful beginning only to fall by the wayside and join the *massa perditionis*. Christ himself suggests this in his parable of the sower (Mark 4:1–9) and the seed, and St. Paul likewise suggests this possibility—even in his own case![11] No realistic account of salvation can

---

11. See 1 Cor 9:27. Paul not only treats as a real possibility that he might be rejected by God, despite all he has done, but clearly indicates that if this were to happen, it would be the consequence of his own unguarded actions. Therefore, he trains and governs himself in order to be able to remain on the path to salvation, just as an athlete does in order to win a race. What Catholics call "mortal sin" can still earn us damnation by short-circuiting the salvation process through ceasing to cooperate with sanctifying grace. This again is a free act on one's own part.

dispense with a discussion of the need for the grace of perseverance, for which sanctifying grace itself bids us to pray.[12]

It is not possible for temptation to overcome God's grace, for evil to conquer good. To the extent that our lives are the product of the operation of God's grace within us, it is not possible for us to backslide or lose our salvation. However, the empirical fact of the matter is that we are constantly tempted and often fall back into our sinful ways. Since this is not a matter of sin overcoming grace, it must be that it is the human will, not yet fully conformed to Christ, which is overcome by temptation and falls. Thus, even though one is in a state of grace, to the extent that the process of sanctification is ongoing and one has not yet been perfected, it is still possible for us to fall from that state of grace and thus lose our salvation. Although we should observe over time that it becomes easier to be good through the influence of God's grace, we must never rest on our laurels or suppose that at any point in our life we are beyond the possibility of being lost. If we do, we do so at our peril. This means that the free cooperation of the human will with grace is ongoing and necessary for us, and since sanctifying grace is not sufficient to prevent our dereliction, we need in addition the grace of perseverance as well.

This grace is acquired through prayer and participation in the life of faith, especially the liturgy and the sacraments, which reinforce and support the commitment we make in the act of faith that follows upon our acquiescence to the operation of the grace of Christ. Again, these religious practices are the means by which the grace of perseverance is distributed to us, not the efficient cause of its being given to us. God has instituted these practices precisely for this purpose and bids us partake of them for our own sakes, not for his. Although we give glory to God in so doing, as we ought to do given God's divine perfection, God does not need our praise and does not command us to praise him in order to feel good about himself, like a petty human ruler or a pompous Cosmic Narcissus. Rather, it is through the effect of these practices in and on our souls that we become more God-like and thus truly glorify him. Like all the acts of God concerning his creatures, God commands that we love him out of love for us, not for himself, and so for our benefit, not his.

---

12. The grace of *final perseverance*—that God should engineer my death at a time when I am in a state of grace in response to my sincere petition to that effect is a "grace" in the sense of a gift from God, but not part of the operation of grace, as I am discussing it here. At the same time, even that sincere petition is the product of the operation of grace.

God, then, is prepared to help us with the ongoing struggle to fight the good fight, run the race, and remain firm in the faith, despite the assaults of doubt and temptation. As such, perseverance is not a matter of pure resolution alone, nor are we left to our own devices. Instead, God has given us the means to remain steadfast in the faith, means that he prompts us to use through sanctifying grace, so that from beginning to end salvation is the work of God. In this instance, God premoves the will in such a way as to prompt us to engage in religious practices designed to confirm us in the faith and blunt the power of doubt and temptation. Again, God's sanctifying grace is sufficient to carry us through if we will only acquiesce to its operation. However, if we forego the necessary means that God has provided for us and instead resolve to trust in our own strength to work out our salvation on our own terms, we will undoubtedly fail. If we do, we have no one to blame but ourselves.

CONCLUSION

I began this chapter with a story intended to serve as an analogy for the plight of the sinner, that of a drowning man saved by an unseen agent who throws him a life ring and pulls him to safety, all the time encouraging him not to give in to the cold and tiredness that motivate him to let go. The drowning man is the sinner, and the saving agent is God. The life ring is the gift of faith, the rope sanctifying grace, and the words of encouragement the grace of perseverance. The analogy is imperfect, since grabbing the life ring is a positive act, and acquiescing in the operation of grace is not and is, indeed, no act at all, not even a negative one. Still, even with the analogy as it stands, we can see that, despite the drowning man's desperate struggle to hang on while he is being pulled to safety, the role that he plays in the story of his rescue is negligible. Even his hanging on in the face of the temptation to give in to cold and tiredness and slip beneath the waves is ultimately made possible only by the encouraging words of his rescuer. Once rescued, the drowning man can hardly claim that he is responsible for that fact or that the life ring is merely a means he uses to save himself. In fact, all credit goes to his rescuer, and the only appropriate response on the part of the drowning man is humble gratitude for the efforts of that rescuer, despite the fact that his own free will played some role in concluding that rescue in circumstances of struggle. The same holds for the sinner saved by grace.

Bibliography

Aquinas, Thomas. *Providence and Predestination*. Translated by Robert W. Mulligan. South Bend, IN: Gateway, 1961.
Aristotle. *The Complete Works of Aristotle*. Edited by Jonathan Barnes. 2 vols. Princeton, NJ: Princeton University Press, 1984.
Augustine of Hippo. *On Free Choice of the Will*. Translated by Thomas Williams. Indianapolis: Hackett, 1994.
Ayers, Michael R. *The Refutation of Determinism*. London: Methuen, 1968.
Barbour, Ian C. *Myths, Models, and Paradigms*. New York: Harper and Row, 1974.
Basinger, David, and Randall Basinger, eds. *Predestination and Free Will*. Downers Grove, IL: IVP, 1986.
Bernard of Clairvaux. *On Grace and Free Will*. Translated by Daniel Donovan. Collegeville, MN?: Cistercian, 1977.
Berofsky, Bernard, ed. *Free Will and Determinism*. New York: Harper and Row, 1966.
Bohm, David. *Causality and Chance in Modern Physics*. Philadelphia: University of Pennsylvania Press, 1957.
Boyle, Joseph M. Jr., Germain Grisez, and Olaf Tollefson. *Free Choice: A Self-Referential Argument*. Notre Dame, IN: Notre Dame University Press, 1976.
Brand, Chad Owen, ed. *Perspectives on Election: Five Views*. Nashville: Broadman and Holman, 2006.
Brand, Myles, ed. *The Nature of Causation*. Urbana: University of Illinois Press, 1976.
Cahalan, John C. *Causal Realism*. Lanham, MD: University Press of America, 1985.
Cahn, Steven M. *Fate, Logic, and Time*. New Haven, CT: Yale University Press, 1967.
Campbell, C. A. *In Defence of Free Will*. London: George Allen and Unwin, 1967.
Churchland, Paul M. "Folk psychology and the explanation of human behavior." In *The Future of Folk Psychology*, edited by John D. Greenwood, 51–69. Cambridge: Cambridge University Press. 1991.
Clarke, Randolph. *Libertarian Accounts of Free Will*. New York: Oxford University Press, 2003.
Cottingham, John, Dugald Murdoch, and Robert Stuthoff, eds. *The Philosophical Writings of Descartes*. 2 vols. Cambridge: Cambridge University Press, 1985.
Cross, Richard. *Duns Scotus*. New York: Oxford University Press, 1999.
Danto, Arthur C. *Analytical Philosophy of Action*. Cambridge: Cambridge University Press, 1973.
Davidson, Donald. *Essays on Actions and Events*. Oxford: Clarendon, 1980.
Dennett, Daniel. *Elbow Room*. Cambridge, MA: MIT Press, 1984.
———. "Two contrasts: folk craft versus folk science, and belief versus opinion." In *The Future of Folk Psychology*, edited by John D. Greenwood, 135–48. Cambridge: Cambridge University Press, 1991.
Denyer, Nicholas. *Time, Action, and Necessity*. London: Duckworth, 1981.

Denzinger, Heinrich. *The Sources of Catholic Doctrine*. 30th ed. Revised by Karl Rahner. St. Louis: Herder, 1954.

Dillenberger, John, ed. *John Calvin: Selections from His Writings*. Garden City, New York: Anchor Books, 1971.

Donagan, Alan. *Choice: The Essential Element in Human Action*. London: Routledge and Kegan Paul, 1987.

Double, Richard. *Metaphilosophy and Free Will*. New York: Oxford University Press, 1996.

———.*The Non-Reality of Free Will*. New York: Oxford University Press, 1991.

Ducasse, Curt John. *Causation and the Types of Necessity*. New York: Dover, 1969.

Duncan, Steven M. *Being, Truth, and Knowledge*. Belmont, CA: Thomson Wadsworth, 2004.

———. "Can I Know What I Am Thinking?" *PhilPapers*, (2011). No pages. Online: http://philpapers.org/.

———. "The Consequences of Neurophysiological Determinism." *PhilPapers* (2011). No pages. Online: http://philpapers.org/.

———. "Could Introspection Be Unreliable—Even in Principle?" *PhilPapers* (2011). No pages. Online: http://philpapers.org/.

———. "Dualism and Neuroscience." *PhilPapers* (2011). No pages. Online: http://philpapers.org/.

———. "Free Will and Luck." *PhilPapers* (2011). No pages. Online: http://philpapers.org/.

———. "Is Neuroscience Possible?" *PhilPapers* (2011). No pages. Online: http://philpapers.org/.

———. *A Primer of Modern Virtue Ethics*. Lanham, MD: University Press of America, 1995.

———. *The Proof of the External World*. Eugene, OR: Wipf and Stock, 2008.

———. "Seeing Other Minds." *PhilPapers* (2011). No pages. Online: http://philpapers.org/.

———. "The Strange Case of Dr. DeVille, or Determinism and Rationality." *PhilPapers* (2011). No pages. Online: http://philpapers.org/.

Dupuis, Jacques. *The Christian Faith*. 7th ed. New York: St. Paul's/Alba House, 2001.

Eccles, John C. *How the Self Controls Its Brain*. Berlin: Springer-Verlag, 1994.

Edwards, Jonathan. *The Freedom of the Will*. Edited by Paul Ramsey. New Haven, CT: Yale University Press, 1957.

———. *The Nature of True Virtue*. Edited by William Frankena. Ann Arbor: University of Michigan Press, 1960.

———. *Selections*. Edited by Charles Faust and Thomas Johnson. New York: Hill and Wang, 1962.

Ellis, Ralph D., and Natika Newton. *How the Mind Uses the Brain*. Chicago: Open Court, 2010.

Emmet, Dorothy. *The Effectiveness of Causes*. Albany: State University of New York Press, 1985.

Fairweather, A. M., ed. *Aquinas on Nature and Grace*. Philadelphia: Westminster Press, 1964.

Farrer, Austin. *Faith and Speculation*. London: A & C Black, 1967.

———.*The Freedom of the Will*. New York: Scribner's, 1957.

———.*The Glass of Vision*. Westminster, UK: Dacre Press, 1948.

Felt, James W., SJ. *Making Sense of Your Freedom*. Ithaca, NY: Cornell University Press, 1994.
Fingarette, Herbert. *Self-Deception*. London: Routledge and Kegan Paul, 1969.
Fischer, John Martin, et al. *Four Views on Free Will*. Oxford: Blackwell, 2007.
Flew, Antony, and Godfrey Vesey. *Agency and Necessity*. Oxford: Basil Blackwell, 1987.
Flint, Thomas. *Divine Providence: The Molinist Account*. Ithaca, NY: Cornell University Press, 1998.
Frank, William B., ed. *Duns Scotus on the Will and Morality*. Translated by Allan B. Wolter. Washington, DC: Catholic University of America Press, 1997.
Garber, Daniel. *Descartes Embodied*. Cambridge: Cambridge University Press, 2001.
Garrigou-LaGrange, Reginald. *Predestination*. St. Louis: B. Herder Book Co., 1939.
Geisler, Norman. *Chosen but Free*. Minneapolis: Bethany House, 1999.
———. *Creating God in the Image of Man?* Minneapolis: Bethany House, 1997.
Ginet, Carl. *On Action*. Cambridge: Cambridge University Press, 1990.
Gleason, Robert W., ed. *The Essential Writings of Pascal*. New York: Mentor-Omega Books, 1966.
Greenwood, John D., ed. *The Future of Folk Psychology*. Cambridge: Cambridge University Press, 1991.
Griffiths, Paul. *Problems of Religious Diversity*. Oxford: Blackwell, 2001.
Grisez, Germain. *Beyond the New Theism*. Notre Dame, IN: Notre Dame University Press, 1975.
Gundry, Stanley N., ed. *Five Views on Sanctification*. Grand Rapids: Zondervan, 1987.
Hampshire, Stuart. *Thought and Action*. London: Chatto and Windus, 1959.
Hardon, John, SJ. *History and Theology of Grace*. Ypsilanti, MI: Veritas Press, 2002.
Hare, John E. *God's Call*. Grand Rapids: Eerdmans, 2001.
———. *The Moral Gap*. Oxford: Clarendon, 1996.
———. *Why Bother Being Good?* Downers Grove, IL: IVP, 2002.
Hartley, David. *Observations on Man*. London: S. Richardson, 1749.
Hesse, Mary. *Models and Analogies in Science*. Notre Dame, IN: Notre Dame University Press, 1966.
Hobbes, Thomas. *Leviathan*. Edited by C. B. McPherson. New York: Pelican Books, 1968.
Honderich, Ted. *How Free Are You?* 2nd ed. New York: Oxford University Press, 2002.
Hook, Sidney, ed. *Determinism and Freedom in the Age of Modern Science*. New York: Colliers, 1958.
Horgan, Terence and James Woodward, "Folk psychology is here to stay." In *The Future of Folk Psychology*, edited by John D. Greenwood, 149–175. Cambridge: Cambridge University Press, 1991.
Hovorun, Cyril. *Will, Action, and Freedom: Christological Controversies in the Seventh Century*. Leiden: Brill Academic, 2008.
Huemer, Michael. *Skepticism and the Veil of Perception*. Lanham, MD: Rowman & Littlefield, 2001.
Journet, Charles. *The Meaning of Grace*. London: Geoffrey Chapman, 1960.
Jowers, Dennis W., and Stanley N. Gundry, eds. *Four Views on Divine Providence*. Grand Rapids: Zondervan, 2011.
Kane, Robert. *Free Will and Values*. Albany: State University of New York Press, 1985.
———. ed., *The Oxford Handbook of Free Will*. New York: Oxford University Press, 2002.

Kant, Immanuel. *Critique of Pure Reason*. Translated by Norman Kemp Smith. New York: St. Martin's, 1929.

———. *Grounding for the Metaphysics of Morals [Grundlegung]*. Translated by James W. Ellington. Indianapolis: Hackett, 1981.

Keathley, Kenneth. *Salvation and Sovereignty: A Molinist Approach*. Nashville: Broadman and Holman, 2010.

Kenny, Anthony. *Aquinas on Mind*. London: Routledge, 1993.

———. *Aristotle's Theory of the Will*. London: Duckworth, 1979.

Kirk, Kenneth E. *The Vision of God*. New York: Harper Torchbooks, 1966.

Lamont, Corliss. *Freedom of Choice Affirmed*. New York: Continuum, 1957.

Langston, Douglas C. *God's Willing Knowledge*. University Park, PA: Penn State University Press, 1986.

Lehrer, Keith. *Freedom and Determinism*. Atlantic Highlands, NJ: Humanities Press, 1966.

Lewis, C. S. *The Abolition of Man*. New York: MacMillan, 1947.

———. *Miracles*. London: Geoffrey Bles, 1947.

Lindberg, David. *Theories of Vision from Al-Kindi to Kepler*. Chicago: University of Chicago Press, 1976.

Locke, John. *An Essay Concerning Human Understanding*. Edited by A. C. Fraser. 2 vols. New York: Dover, 1959.

Lonergan, Bernard. *Grace and Freedom: Operative Grace in the Thought of St. Thomas Aquinas*. Toronto: University of Toronto Press, 2000.

Lowe, E. J. *Personal Agency*. New York: Oxford University Press, 2008.

Lucas, John. *The Freedom of the Will*. Oxford: Clarendon, 1970.

Mackie, J. L. *The Cement of the Universe*. Oxford: Clarendon, 1974.

Malebranche, Nicolas. *Treatise on Nature and Grace*. Oxford: Clarendon, 1992.

Margolis, Joseph. "The autonomy of folk psychology." In *The Future of Folk Psychology*, edited by John D. Greenwood, 242–62. Cambridge: Cambridge University Press, 1991.

Maritain, Jacques. *God and the Permission of Evil*. Milwaukee: Bruce Publishing, 1966.

McClain, Michael, and W. Mark Richardson, eds. *Human and Divine Agency*. Lanham, MD: University Press of America, 1999.

McDonough, Richard. "A culturalist account of folk psychology." In *The Future of Folk Psychology*, edited by John D. Greenwood, 263–88. Cambridge: Cambridge University Press, 1991.

McGinn, Colin. *The Mysterious Flame*. New York, Basic Books, 1999.

McGrath, Alister E. *Iustitia Dei: A History of the Christian Doctrine of Justification*. 3rd ed. Cambridge: Cambridge University Press, 2005.

Mead, George Herbert. *Selected Writings*. Edited by Andrew J. Reck. Indianapolis: Bobbs-Merrill, 1964.

Melden, A. I. *Free Action*. London: Routledge and Kegan Paul, 1961.

Mele, Alfred. *Effective Intentions*. New York, Oxford, 2009.

———. *Free Will and Luck*. New York: Oxford, 2006.

Morgenbesser, Sidney, and James Walsh, eds. *Free Will*. Englewood Cliffs, NJ: Prentice-Hall, 1962.

Morris, Thomas V. *Divine and Human Action*. Ithaca, NY: Cornell University Press, 1988.

Most, William G. *Grace, Predestination, and the Salvific Will of God.* Front Royal, VA: Christendom, 1992.
Nagel, Thomas. *The Last Word.* New York: Oxford University Press, 1997.
———. *Mortal Questions*, New York: Cambridge University Press, 1979.
———. *The View from Nowhere.* New York: Oxford University Press, 1986.
The New American Bible. New York: Oxford, 1995.
O'Connor, D. J. *Free Will.* New York: Anchor Doubleday, 1971.
O'Connor, Timothy. *Persons and Causes.* New York: Oxford University Press, 2002.
Pereboom, Derk. *Living Without Free Will.* Cambridge: Cambridge University Press, 2006.
Peterson, Robert A., and Michael D. Williams. *Why I Am Not an Arminian.* Downers Grove, IL: IVP, 2004.
Pieper, Josef. *The Concept of Sin.* Translated by Edward T. Oakes. South Bend, IN: St. Augustine's Press, 2001.
———. *Reality and the Good.* Translated by Stella Lange. Chicago: Regnery, 1967.
Pinnock, Clark H. *The Grace of God and the Will of Man.* Minneapolis: Bethany House, 1989.
Pinson, Matthew, and Stanley N. Gundry, eds. *Four Views on Eternal Security.* Grand Rapids: Zondervan, 2002.
Plato. *Complete Works.* Edited by John M. Cooper. Indianapolis: Hackett, 1997.
Pohle, Joseph, and Arthur Preuss. *Grace: Actual and Habitual.* St. Louis: B. Herder Book Co., 1914.
Pontifex, Dom Mark. *Freedom and Providence.* New York: Hawthorn Books, 1960.
Ramsey, William, Stephen Stich, and Joseph Garon. "Connectionism, eliminativism, and the future of folk psychology." In *The Future of Folk Psychology*, edited by John D. Greenwood, 93–119. Cambridge: Cambridge University Press, 1991.
Rickaby, Joseph. *Free Will and Four English Philosophers.* London: Burns and Oates, 1906.
Rogers, Katharin. *Anselm on Freedom.* Oxford: Clarendon, 2008.
Rowe, William L. *Thomas Reid on Freedom and Morality.* Ithaca, NY: Cornell University Press, 1991.
Searle, John. *Mind: An Introduction.* New York: Oxford University Press, 2005.
———. *Minds, Brains, and Science.* Cambridge, MA: Harvard University Press, 1984.
———. *The Rediscovery of the Mind.* Cambridge, MA: MIT Press, 1992.
Sehon, Scott. *Teleological Realism.* Cambridge, MA: MIT Press, 2005.
Sellars, Wilfred. *Science, Perception, and Reality.* London: Routledge and Kegan Paul, 1960.
Shapiro, Lisa, ed. and trans. *The Correspondence between Princess Elisabeth of Bohemia and René Descartes.* Chicago: University of Chicago Press, 2007.
Simon, Yves. *Freedom of Choice.* New York: Fordham University Press, 1969.
Skirry, Justin. *Descartes and the Metaphysics of Human Nature.* London: Continuum, 2005.
Smilansky, Saul. *Free Will and Illusion.* New York: Oxford University Press, 2002.
Smith, A. D. *The Problem of Perception.* Cambridge, MA: Harvard University Press, 2002.
Sosa, Ernest, ed. *Causation and Conditionals.* London: Oxford University Press, 1975.
Strawson, Peter. *Individuals.* New York: Anchor Books, 1959.

Styles, Elizabeth. *The Psychology of Attention*. Hove, East Sussex, UK: Psychology Press, 1997.
Suarez, Francisco. *On Creation, Conservation, and Concurrence*. Translated by Alfred J. Freddoso. South Bend, IN: St. Augustine's Press, 2002.
———. *On Efficient Causality*. Translated by Alfred J. Freddoso. New Haven, CT: Yale University Press, 1994.
———. *On the Essence of Finite Being*. Translated by Norman J. Wells. Milwaukee: Marquette University Press, 1983.
Swinburne, Richard. *The Existence of God*. 2nd ed. Oxford: Clarendon, 2004.
Tappan, Henry P. *The Doctrine of the Will, Applied to Moral Agency and Responsibility*. New York: Wiley and Putnam, 1841.
———. *The Doctrine of the Will, Determined by an Appeal to Consciousness*. New York: Wiley and Putnam, 1840.
Tekippe, Terry J. *Lonergan and Thomas on the Will*. Lanham, MD: University Press of America, 1993.
Thorp, John. *Free Will: A Defence against Neurophysiological Determinism*. London: Routledge and Kegan Paul, 1980.
Titchener, Edward Bradford. *Lectures on the Elementary Psychology of Feeling and Attention*. New York: MacMillan, 1908.
Tolkien, J. R. R. *The Silmarillion*. New York, Houghton Mifflin, 1977.
Tracy, Thomas, ed. *The God Who Acts*. University Park, PA: Penn State University Press, 1994.
Turretin, Francis. *Justification*. Edited by James T. Dennison Jr. Phillipsburg, NJ: Presbyterian and Reformed Publishing, 1993.
Van Inwagen, Peter. *An Essay on Free Will*. Oxford: Clarendon, 1983.
Vos, Arvin. *Aquinas, Calvin, and Contemporary Protestant Thought*. Grand Rapids: Eerdmans, 1985.
Walls, Jerry L., and Joseph R. Dongell. *Why I Am Not a Calvinist*. Downers Grove, IL: IVP, 2004.
Ware, Bruce, ed. *Perspectives on the Doctrine of God: Four Views*. Nashville: Broadman and Holman, 2001.
Watson, Gary, ed. *Free Will*, 2nd ed., Oxford: Oxford University Press, 2003.
Wegner, Daniel. *The Illusion of Conscious Will*. Cambridge, MA: MIT Press, 2003.
White, Alan R. *Attention*. Oxford: Basil Blackwell, 1964.
———. *The Philosophy of Action*. London: Oxford University Press, 1968.
Wilson, George M. *The Intentionality of Human Action*. Stanford, CA: Stanford University Press, 1989.
Winter, Ernst F., ed. and trans. *Erasmus–Luther: Discourse on Free Will*. New York: Frederick Ungar, 1961.
Wojtyla, Karel (Pope John Paul II). *The Acting Person*. Dordrecht, Holland: Reidel, 1979.
Wright, N. T. (Tom). *Justification: God's Plan and Paul's Vision*. London: SPCK, 2009.

www.ingramcontent.com/pod-product-compliance
Lightning Source LLC
Chambersburg PA
CBHW071858160426
43197CB00013B/2519